SILK PAINTING & BATIK PROJECT BOOK

Using wax and paint to create inspired decorative items for the home, with 35 projects shown in 300 easy-to-follow photographs

SUSIE STOKOE

southwater

This edition is published by Southwater, an imprint of Anness Publishing Ltd, 108 Great Russell Street, London WC1B 3NA; info@anness.com

www.southwaterbooks.com; www.annesspublishing.com; twitter: @Anness_Books

If you like the images in this book and would like to investigate using them for publishing, promotions or advertising, please visit our website www.practicalpictures.com for more information.

© Anness Publishing Ltd 2015

A CIP catalogue record for this book is available from the British Library.

Publisher: Joanna Lorenz
Editorial Director: Helen Sudell
Project Editor: Simona Hill
Photographers: Nicki Dowey, Rodney Forte, John Freeman, Michelle Garrett, Debbie Patterson, Adrian Taylor and Mark Wood
Designer: Nigel Partridge
Production Controller: Rosanna Anness

PUBLISHER'S NOTE

A few basic safety rules should be followed when working with dyes. Label all solutions and keep them away from children and animals. Do not eat or drink while using dyes, and wash your hands before handling food. If you spill dye powder, sweep up as much as possible before washing with plenty of water. Blot up spilt dye solution with newspaper, then wash down. Remove dye stains from hard surfaces with household cleaner or diluted bleach.

Although the advice and information in this book are believed to be accurate and true at the time of going to press, neither the authors nor the publisher can accept any legal responsibility or liability for any errors or omissions that may have been made nor for any inaccuracies nor for any loss, harm or injury that comes about from following instructions or advice in this book.

SILK PAINTING
& BATIK PROJECT BOOK

Contents

Introduction

Decorating silk and cotton with a variety of paints, inks and dyes is fun and easy to do. You can use the decorated fabric to make scarves, ties, cushions,

shawls and wallhangings. There are many methods

of painting silk, and you do not have to be an artist to achieve beautiful results.

This book shows you how to paint with iron-fix (set) silk paints and gutta, and how to use salt and bleach to create interesting effects on fabric. Silk and other natural fabrics, such as cotton and leather, can also be used in batik. Batik involves applying hot wax to the surface of fabric, cracking it when cool, and immersing the fabric in dye to create delicate patterns of lines on the fabric. The wax is applied either with a brush or with a traditional Indonesian tool known as a tjanting.

As well as explaining and illustrating the techniques involved in silk painting and batik, this book contains over 35 step-by-step projects. Each project

has a symbol indicating its level of difficulty. The symbol ⌇ indicates that a

project is simple to do. Projects with the symbol ⌇⌇⌇⌇ require an advanced

level of skill to complete. Following these symbols, you can begin with a salt-

patterned greetings card or batik napkin and progress to a multi-coloured

batik cushion cover, or a double-panelled room

divider made from lengths of painted silk.

There are plenty of templates included here to

use as the basis for your designs, but as you grow

more confident, you may want to create your own.

Some of the most striking designs are the simplest.

A repeating pattern of squares or dots can look

most effective in toning colours. The charm of

handmade fabrics is their spontaneity, so do not

worry too much about perfection. If you are unsure

of your skills, practise first on a piece of spare fabric or dye several pieces of

fabric in a dye bath and choose the best to assemble the project. Colourful

remnants and test pieces can always be made into gifts such as a pretty

handkerchief or lavender bag.

So whether you are an enthusiastic beginner or

already skilled in both crafts and looking for inspi-

ration, you have here an invaluable sourcebook of

techniques and ideas.

Painting on Silk

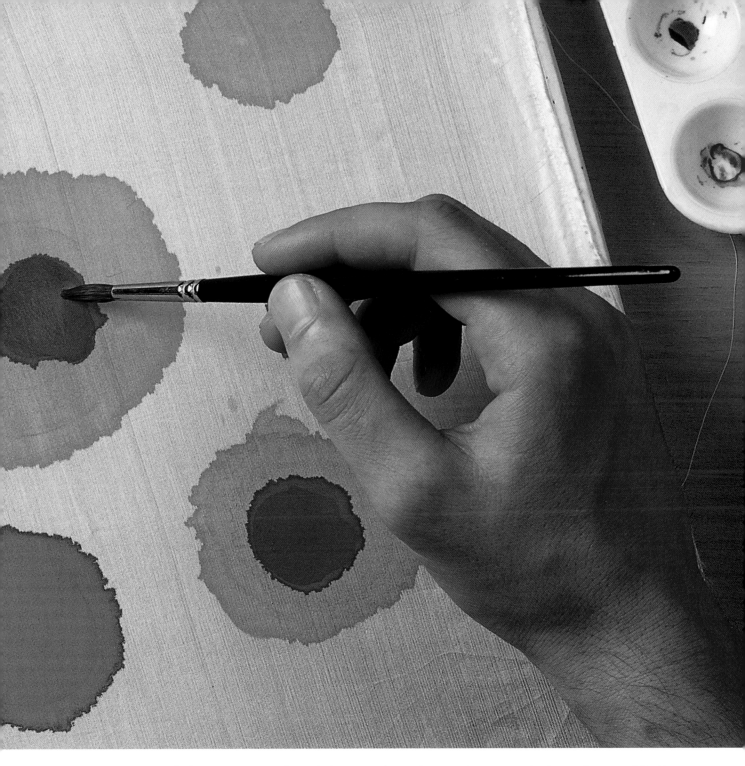

Silk is the ideal fabric to work with. It absorbs paints and dyes beautifully, and there is a special range of transparent iron-fix (set) paints designed to give lovely clear colours. Create finely drawn designs using gutta – an outline that creates a barrier to prevent the paint from spreading – or experiment with abstract effects by adding unusual materials such as salt and bleach.

Hand-crafted Art

Archaeological evidence tells us that silk was culti-vated in China as early as 3200BC, using the finest silkworm caterpillars fed on the best mulberry leaves. The Chinese kept the making of this luxury fabric a closely guarded secret, trading silk with other countries for precious stones and metals. Eventually silk reached the Roman Empire, transported along the famous "Silk Road" via northern India. The Romans at first paid outrageous prices for this highly desirable fabric.

Silk is the most beautiful of all fabrics and an ideal surface for painting on.

Its sensual feel, lustre and ability to absorb colour have inspired artists throughout the centuries. It is available in different weights, from fine, floating georgette and chiffon to heavy habotai or pongee, so you can choose the ideal fabric for each project.

A range of transparent iron-fix (set) silk paints has been specially designed for use with silk alone. The colours are set by heat, so you can use an iron or a hairdryer, which is useful for projects such as a parasol where ironing would

be impractical. To draw precise designs on silk, transparent or coloured gutta is often used as a resist to prevent the paint from flowing across the fabric into unwanted areas. The transparent gutta is removed at the end by hand washing, while the coloured gutta remains on the fabric as part of the finished design. Wash silk

by hand with a mild detergent and press it on the reverse side while it is still damp.

If you are not a proficient artist, you can draw a design first on paper or trace one of the templates at the back of the book, then transfer it on to the silk using a vanishing fabric marker. Wonderful effects can also be created by sprinkling different kinds of salt on to the damp silk paints.

Another technique is to remove the colour from pre-dyed silk with bleach, dotted over the surface with a paintbrush, which gives a subtle effect and different colour density. Finally, machine or hand embroidery threads will add three-dimensional texture to your individually painted work of art.

Although any fabric paint can be used on silk, specially formulated silk paints are the best choice. Many weights and types of silk can be used, with medium-weight habotai silk being a good choice for beginners.

Materials

Paper

Silk paints can be fixed by placing each painted area between sheets of paper and ironing.

Powder dye

Fabrics can be pre-dyed using hot or cold powder dyes.

Salt

Add to damp silk paint to distort the colours. Brush off after use.

Silk

Available in different weights. Crêpe de chine, chiffon and georgette are ideal for lightweight items. Habotai or pongee silk varies in weight and has a smooth, soft sheen, as does silk-satin.

Sticky-backed plastic (Contact paper)

Attach to thin cardboard stencils and cut out to stick temporarily on to fabric to resist the paint.

Thickener

Mix into silk paints to prevent them from spreading. Thickened paint is used for painting details.

Watercolours or coloured inks

Useful for preparing designs on paper as they have the same quality as transparent silk paints on silk. Their strong colours can easily be seen through silk.

Anti-spreading agent

Starch-like liquid applied to fabric to prevent the paints from spreading. Remove by hand washing.

Batik wax

Can be used to resist silk paints. Heat the wax in a double boiler or wax pot.

Bleach

Apply to pre-dyed fabric to remove the colour. Wash out immediately.

Gutta

Gel-like substance used with an applicator to draw a design on silk. It acts as a barrier to the paint. Remove transparent gutta by hand washing.

Iron-fix (set) silk paints

These paints are specially designed for use on silk. They are fixed (set) by direct heat, such as an iron or a hairdryer. Steam-fix dyes are also available, and are fixed with steam.

Silk painting does require specialist equipment, but most of it is quite inexpensive. The most important pieces you will need are a wooden painting frame and silk pins to hold the delicate fabric on the frame.

Equipment

Craft knife
Use to cut stencils. Always use with a cutting mat.

Double boiler or wax pot
Use to melt batik wax.

Gutta applicator
Fitted with various-size nibs (tips) for drawing a design on to silk to resist the paint. Fill no more than three-quarters full for even, flowing paint.

Hairdryer
Use to fix (set) iron-fix silk paints.

Iron
Use to press the fabric, and to make iron-fix silk paint permanent.

Masking tape
Use to mask off areas of the design.

Needle
Use for hand stitching.

Paint palette
Use to hold and mix paint colours.

Paintbrushes
Use a decorator's paintbrush to paint large areas. Use a medium paintbrush to paint a design, and a fine paintbrush for details. Use a sponge brush to dampen silk before painting and to apply paint or anti-spreading agent. Use a toothbrush to spray paint.

Pens and pencils
Use a black marker pen to draw on the acetate sheet. Use a soft pencil to trace templates.

Silk-painting frame
Make your own wooden frame to stretch silk taut ready for painting.

Silk pins (push pins)
Use special flat-headed pins with three points to attach silk to a frame.

Sponge
A natural sponge can be used to apply paint, e.g. around stencils.

Staple gun
Use to mount a picture in a frame.

Tailor's chalk/Fabric marker
Use to temporarily mark designs on to the fabric.

Silk fibres normally contain dressing that looks slightly oily. It needs to be removed from the silk before painting or dyeing so that the colours can penetrate the fibres. To remove the dressing, hand wash the silk in warm, soapy water, using a mild detergent. Dry it by hanging it on a line, or roll it in a towel to remove excess water. Press while damp. Some objects, such as fans and umbrellas, are unwashable, and these should be painted by incorporating a thickener into the paint. Start with a simple project and practise with the silk paints first.

Techniques

Making a frame

Several different kinds of silk-painting frame are available for purchase, the adjustable ones being the most useful.

1 Cut four pieces of planed timber or battening to make a frame. The frame should be slightly larger than the finished piece, to allow for trimming untidy fabric edges. Using wood adhesive, glue two pieces together to form a right angle. Repeat with the remaining two pieces and leave the adhesive to dry.

◀ **2** When the adhesive has set, glue the two right angles together to form the frame. Leave the glue to dry, then tap a panel pin (tack) into each joint to hold it firmly.

Pinning silk to a frame

Silk should be pulled taut on a frame and be springy to the touch before it is painted on, to ensure an even coverage of paint.

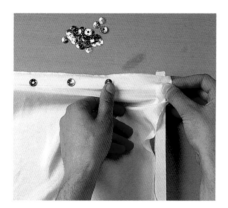

1 Use three-pronged silk pins to attach the silk to the frame. Place the first pin in the centre of one edge and work out towards each corner.

2 Space the pins an equal distance apart. Pull the silk over the frame and pin the opposite edge, placing the pins directly opposite each other.

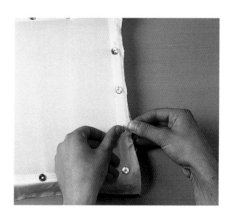

3 Pin down one of the sides, pull the silk taut across the frame, and then pin the final side. The silk should be springy, without being too tight.

Paint effects

Iron-fix (set) silk paints are available in a wide range of colours and are specially designed for use with silk.

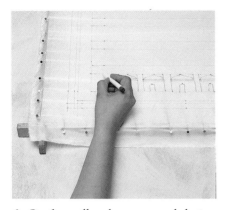

1 On fine silks place a traced design underneath the frame and copy over it with a vanishing marker pen.

2 Or, turn the frame upside down and trace the design with a pencil. On the right side, trace the lines with gutta.

3 Mix paints together to achieve the exact shade required. Ensure you have enough of each for the whole design.

4 A single paint colour mixed with white produces a delicate pastel tone. Continue adding white until you achieve the desired colour.

5 Paints can be diluted with water to make a wash. This is most often used to fill a background. Use a large brush to apply the diluted paint quickly over a large area.

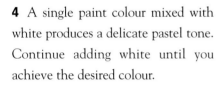
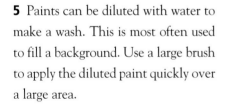

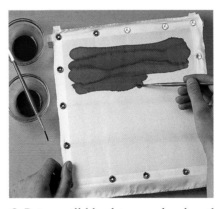

6 Paints will bleed into each other if applied quickly before they dry. Use a soft brush and flowing movements.

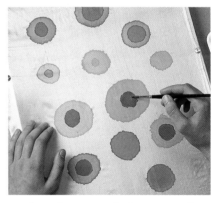

7 If a colour is applied over another, while the first paint is damp, they will merge and give a soft, blurred effect.

8 When using gutta, dot paint in the centre of each outlined shape and it will quickly spread to the gutta lines.

9 Use a large brush (sponge brush or paint brush) to fill large areas quickly. This will stop watermarks from appearing. Use a fine brush for details.

10 Use a cotton wool ball held between tweezers or a clothes peg (pin) to create a softer tool where no definition is required.

Using gutta

Gutta is a thin, gel-like substance that acts as a barrier against paints, isolating areas of colour. It is applied to the fabric using an applicator that can be fitted with a detachable nib (tip) according to the fineness of line required. Do not fill the applicator more than three-quarters full and squeeze gently. Alternatively, purchase gutta in ready-to-use tubes.

Gutta is available in various colours, as well as transparent. Transparent guttas wash out, but coloured ones need to be fixed (set) and remain as part of the finished design. When working with gutta, it is essential to use special silk paints, as ordinary fabric paints contain binders that leave the colour opaque and can stiffen the fabric.

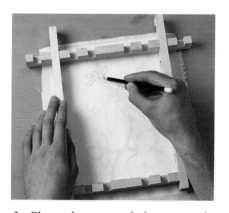

1 Place the covered frame upside down on the design and trace the pattern on to the back of the fabric, using a soft pencil. This will reverse the design; if you wish the design to be the original way round, transfer it first on to tracing paper.

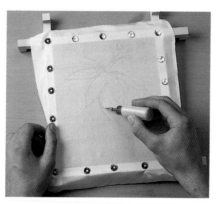

2 Working on the right side of the silk, go over the design outline with gutta. It is important to maintain a continuous line, otherwise the paints will be able to seep through. Turn the silk over from time to time to check the back. Here, the applicator is fitted with a fine detachable nib (tip). Leave to dry.

3 When the gutta is dry, apply the silk paints in the centre of each defined area. Keep the brushstrokes light, allowing the colour to bleed from the brush outwards to the gutta lines. If the paint breaks through the gutta line there is no way to remedy the situation, except by washing the silk and starting again.

Fixing (setting) silk paints

Iron-fix (set) silk paints are made permanent by the use of heat, either by ironing the fabric or by using a hairdryer.

1 When the painting is complete, leave the paints to dry.

▸**2** Remove the finished piece from the frame and fix (set) the paints, following the manufacturer's instructions, usually by pressing with a warm, dry iron on the wrong side.

3 Alternatively, use a hairdryer set on a high setting to fix (set) a piece of silk that is still mounted on a silk-painting frame, or if the object would be difficult to iron.

4 Wash out transparent guttas by hand, using a mild detergent.

Using thickeners

There are two types of thickener, both of which are used to prevent the silk paints from spreading into unwanted areas of the design. Thickener allows you to paint without flooding the fabric. It is used on objects that cannot be pre-washed, or where you are working with a stencil and do not want the paint to seep underneath. Thickened paint is mostly used for painting small areas and to add details to some designs. Mix thickener into the paints by placing both together in a screw-top jar with a lid and shaking vigorously.

1 Use thickener for painting small areas and to add details.

2 Alternatively apply anti-spreading agent to the silk before painting.

Using salt

Designs can be created by sprinkling salt or dabbing bleach on to the surface of the fabric while the paints are damp. Adding salt to damp silk paint will distort the paint, giving a lovely mottled effect. Different salts will produce different results, so experiment with different kinds. It is important that the paint is still damp when you add the salt, so alternate painting and applying salt. Leave the finished design to dry naturally, then gently rub off the salt crystals.

1 Add rock salt grains with tweezers.

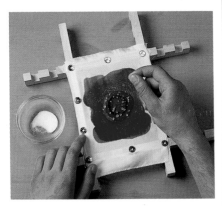

2 Sprinkle fine salt over the surface.

Using bleach

Remove the colour from pre-dyed silk by bleaching using a brush.

Dye the silk as desired, following the manufacturer's instructions. Apply the bleach a little at a time until you get the desired effect. Wash the silk immediately to remove the bleach, otherwise it will rot the fabric.

Trace this pretty flower motif on to a delicate silk camisole or pyjama top, then paint it in a soft pastel colour. Simple machine embroidery stitches complete the fresh, natural design.

Flowery Camisole

you will need
tracing paper and pencil
white paper
silk camisole, pre-washed
shallow cardboard box
vanishing fabric marker
silk pins (push pins)
transparent gutta and applicator
fine artist's paintbrush
paint palette
small bowl
iron-fix (set) silk paints, in 1 colour
and white
iron
sewing machine
metallic thread

1 Trace the floral motifs from the back of the book on to a sheet of paper. Separate the two sides of the camisole by placing a shallow cardboard box inside. Insert the paper on top of the box and trace several flowers on to the outside of the camisole, using a vanishing fabric marker.

2 To make the silk taut, pin the camisole to the sides of the box, through the seams or hem only, using silk pins. Smooth out any wrinkles. Apply transparent gutta along the outlines of the design, making sure there are no gaps in the line. Leave the gutta to dry thoroughly.

3 Using a fine artist's paintbrush and a paint palette, mix the coloured paint with white until you achieve the desired tone. Apply the paint within the gutta outline. Allow the paint to dry thoroughly, then unpin the silk from the box.

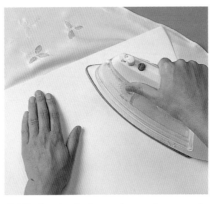

4 To fix (set) the colour, place each painted area between two sheets of white paper and press using a warm, dry iron, following the manufacturer's instructions. Hand wash the camisole to remove the gutta.

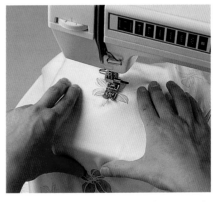

5 Thread a sewing machine with metallic thread. Holding the fabric taut with your hands, stitch two straight lines as a stem for each flower. Add any other details you like.

Transform a silk tie with coloured stripes and spots. The stripes are painted with a makeshift tool made from a clothes peg (pin) and a cotton wool ball, and the spots are made by adding rock salt to the silk.

Salt-painted Tie

you will need

plain-weave silk tie, white or very pale, pre-washed

transparent gutta and applicator

cotton ball

clothes peg (pin)

iron-fix (set) silk paints, in 2 colours

rock salt

tweezers

medium artist's paintbrush

iron

1 Place the tie face down on the work surface. Draw a line with transparent gutta right round the reverse side, about 1cm/½in from the edge. This will prevent the paints from spreading round to the back.

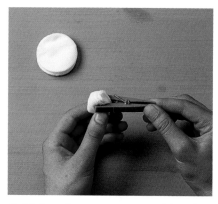

2 Make a large painting tool by clipping a cotton ball into a clothes peg (pin), as shown.

3 Using the first paint colour, apply a stripe of paint across the width of the tie front. While the paint is still damp, place evenly spaced salt crystals along the strip, using tweezers. Continue to apply paint and salt in this way down the length of the tie. When the tie is completely covered, leave it to dry for at least 20 minutes.

4 Using an artist's paintbrush, apply horizontal stripes in the second paint colour between the lines of salt. Leave to dry for 20 minutes.

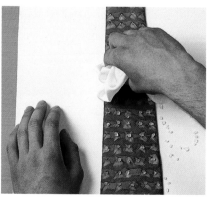

5 When the tie is dry, gently remove the salt crystals. Rock salt comes away quite easily, but smaller salt grains may stick. If this happens, gently rub the tie on itself and the grains will fall away. Iron the tie to fix (set) the paints, following the manufacturer's instructions, then wash it to remove the gutta and press again.

Simple flower stencils show up against a background of gently spotted colour, sprayed with a toothbrush. Practise the spraying technique first on paper to get the desired effect.

Patterned Seat Cover

you will need

chair with removable padded seat
paper and pencil
scissors
silk pins (push pins)
silk crêpe de chine, pre-washed
silk-painting frame
vanishing fabric marker
sponge brush
anti-spreading agent
tracing paper
thin cardboard
sticky-backed plastic (contact paper)
iron-fix (set) silk paint
small bowl
old toothbrush
white paper
iron
staple gun

1 Remove the padded seat from the chair, place it on a piece of paper and draw round it. Add a 5cm/2in seam allowance all round and cut out the shape. Pin the crêpe de chine to a silk-painting frame. Place the seat template on top and draw round it with a vanishing fabric marker.

2 Using a sponge brush, coat the fabric with anti-spreading agent. Trace the templates from the back of the book, transfer them to thin cardboard and cut out. Place each on sticky-backed plastic (contact paper) and draw around the shapes. Cut out approximately ten of each shape.

3 Peel away the paper backing and stick the shapes on to the fabric to form a pattern. Pour a little paint into a bowl.

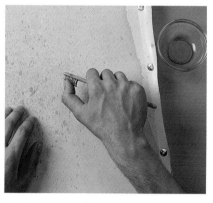

4 Dip a toothbrush in paint, and lightly spray it over the fabric. Leave to dry, then peel off the plastic shapes. Sandwich the fabric between sheets of white paper and iron to fix (set) the colour. Hand wash and dry. Stretch it over the seat and attach it to the underside, using a staple gun.

Paint stripes of colour, then spoon on lines of salt while the silk is still damp to create a soft, watery effect. Alternate the painting and the salt, rather than painting the whole area first.

Abstract Picture Frame

you will need

silk pins (push pins)

at least 30cm/12in square lightweight plain-weave silk, pre-washed

silk-painting frame

iron-fix (set) silk paints

small bowls

fine artist's paintbrushes

small spoon

fine table salt

iron

pencil and ruler

graph paper

craft knife and cutting mat

PVA (white) glue

mounting board

wadding (batting)

scissors

adhesive tape

dressmaker's pins

needle

matching sewing thread

4 small ribbon rose decorations

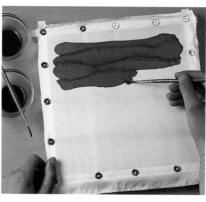

1 Pin the silk to the frame, pulling the fabric taut. Paint a few stripes of alternate colours, making the stripes at least 2.5cm/1in wide.

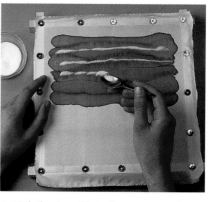

2 While the silk is damp, spoon lines of salt grains along the stripes. Continue alternating paint and salt until the surface is covered. Leave to dry. Brush off the salt, remove the silk from the frame and iron to fix (set) the paints.

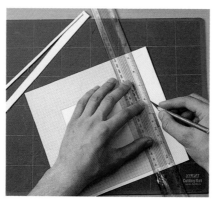

3 Cut out a 20cm/8in square from graph paper. Draw a 10cm/4in square centrally within it and cut out. Glue the paper to mounting board and cut out with a craft knife.

4 Centre the frame on a 25cm/10in square of wadding (batting). Trim off the corners of the wadding, then fold and stick the surplus down with adhesive tape. Cut an "x" across the central square of wadding, trim to 2cm/¾in, turn back over the frame edges and tape down.

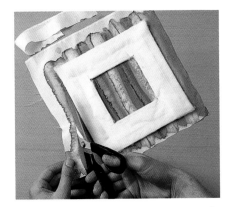

5 Pin the silk with the wrong side against the wadding. Trim the excess fabric to 3cm/1¼in. Cut an "x" in the silk inside the frame. Trim to 3cm/1¼in. Fold the corners over the back, fold the flaps in and stitch the joins.

6 Wrap the inner edges over the frame and lace them to the outer edges with long stitches. Do not pull the silk too tightly or the shape will distort. Stitch a small ribbon rose to each inside corner of the frame.

7 Cut a 20cm/8in square of mounting board to make the backing. Cut a tall, right-angled triangle, score along the longest side 1cm/½in from the edge and bend it over to make a stand. Trim the bottom edge and check it will stand properly. Glue the stand to the backing, starting from the bottom edge. Attach the backing to the frame by gluing along three sides, leaving one side free so that a picture can be slipped inside. To make the picture permanent, add the picture before gluing all four sides and attaching the backing. Leave the glue to dry.

Make good use of a spare scrap of silk by creating your own handmade card. Use a ready-made greetings card frame with a window cut in it, or mount the silk panels on handmade paper as in the main picture.

Salt-patterned Greetings Card

you will need

silk pins (push pins)

lightweight silk, pre-washed

small silk-painting frame

greetings card frame

soft pencil

iron-fix (set) silk paints

fine artist's paintbrushes

small bowls

rock salt and fine table salt

iron

scissors

spray adhesive (stencil mount)

scrap paper

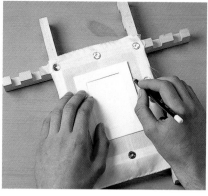

1 Pin the silk on to the silk-painting frame. Place the greetings card frame centrally on the silk and draw round it, using a soft pencil.

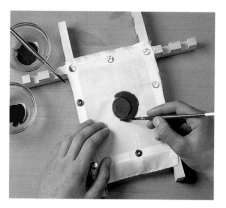

2 Begin to paint an abstract design on the silk within the drawn square. When first learning this technique, it is a good idea to confine your designs to simple spots, stripes, geometric shapes and patterns.

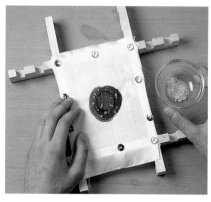

3 While the fabric is still damp with paint but not wet, drop on some rock salt. Build up the design by alternating painting and sprinkling salt. Use different-sized salt crystals, such as rock salt and fine table salt, to create an interesting pattern. Leave to dry completely – this should take about 20 minutes.

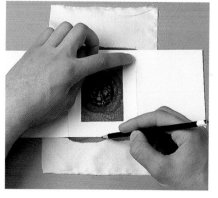

4 Remove the silk from the frame and brush the salt from the surface. Fix (set) the paint by pressing with an iron. Open the card and place the frame over the painted silk. Use a soft pencil to draw on the silk along the top and bottom edge of the card, indicating where the folds of the card fall. Close the card and draw the fold lines on the silk.

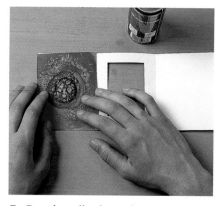

5 Cut the silk along the lines. Open the card and cover the section to the left of the frame with spray adhesive (stencil mount), protecting the rest of the card with scrap paper. Mount the fabric on the adhesive and trim any excess silk. Lightly spray the back of the frame with adhesive, then fold the card so that the silk is sandwiched in the frame.

Transform a small silk umbrella into an exquisite parasol by adding a freehand design outlined with dots of metallic fabric paint. Open the umbrella while you are working so that the silk is stretched taut.

Summer Parasol

you will need

small plain silk umbrella

sponge brush

fabric paints in 4 colours, including metallic

hairdryer

tailor's chalk

fine artist's paintbrushes

1 Apply a background colour to some or all of the umbrella panels. Dampen the silk using a sponge brush soaked in water then apply the paint using the sponge brush. Fix (set) the paint with a hairdryer used on a high heat.

2 Using tailor's chalk, draw your choice of design on to the umbrella. Refer to the template provided. Using a paintbrush, apply dots of metallic paint along some of the tailor's chalk outlines. Allow to dry.

3 Paint a line along one edge of some of the chalked leaves. Paint in the details of the leaves in a contrasting colour. Add simple stylized flowers as desired. Leave to dry. Remove the tailor's chalk by brushing the surface lightly. Fix the paint using the heat of a hairdryer.

Decorate a plain silk fan with a lovely floral design in paint and gold gutta. In case adhesive has been used in the manufacture of the fan, add thickener to the paints to prevent them from spreading.

Painted Fan

you will need

pencil

plain silk fan

paper

tracing paper

masking tape

vanishing fabric marker (optional)

gold gutta

gutta applicator fitted with a

fine nib (tip)

thickener

iron-fix (set) silk paints

small bowls

fine artist's paintbrushes

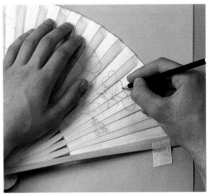

1 Draw around the open fan on to a piece of paper, marking a dotted line where the fabric starts on the fan's handle. Trace the template from the back of the book, and transfer it to paper, within the outline of the fan.

2 Secure the open fan on top of the design with masking tape. Trace the flowers lightly on to the fan, using a soft pencil or vanishing fabric marker. Trace over the design with gold gutta. Leave to dry.

3 The gum used to make the fan may prevent the gutta from acting as a barrier, so mix thickener into the paints to keep them from spreading. Paint the design, using light brushstrokes. To keep the colours clean, use a different brush for each colour. If you need to wash a brush, make sure it is dry before using it again, to prevent the paints becoming too watery.

An abstract geometric design makes a highly unusual clock, with a ready-made clock movement and hands attached in the centre. Heavy habotai silk is ideal for this project.

Silk Clock Face

you will need

heavyweight habotai silk, pre-washed
silk-painting frame
silk pins (push pins)
black felt-tipped pen
tracing paper
masking tape
vanishing fabric marker
metallic gutta and applicator
iron-fix (set) silk paints
palette
paintbrushes
white paper
iron
scissors
heavy cardboard
rubber-based glue
fine braid
clock movement and hands

3 Apply the metallic gutta over the outline of the design, then leave to dry thoroughly.

1 Stretch the silk on to the frame and pin in position. The fabric must be absolutely taut. Trace the template at the back of the book, in felt-tipped pen, allowing for a generous border all around the design.

4 Apply the silk paints, taking care not to splash or go over any lines of gutta. Paint in the design. Leave the fabric to dry before removing it from the frame.

2 Secure the tracing paper underneath the silk frame with pieces of masking tape at each corner. Turn the silk frame over and draw on to the silk with the vanishing fabric marker, going over the design below.

5 Place the painted silk between two sheets of clean white paper and iron it, according to the manufacturer's instructions, to fix (set) the paint. To assemble the clock, cut two pieces of cardboard to the size of the finished design. Glue them together to form the base for the silk and leave under a heavy object to dry for 24 hours.

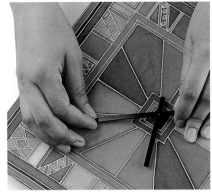

7 Cut a piece of silk slightly smaller than the block and stick it on to the back of the block to cover the joins and neaten the edges. Trim the edges with fine braid.

6 Trim the edges of the silk slightly larger than the cardboard. Centre the cardboard block on the silk and glue in place, stretching the silk to fit.

8 Make a hole in the centre of the design and attach the clock movement and hands.

Simple circles of contrasting colours decorate this unusual ornament, inspired by exquisite Chinese silk kites. It is intended for decorative use, to hang on the wall as you would a picture.

Polka Dot Kite

you will need

silk pins (push pins)

150 x 120cm/60 x 48in silk, pre-washed

silk-painting frame

iron-fix (set) silk paints

fine artist's paintbrushes

paint palette

iron

sewing machine and sewing thread

scissors

fine ribbons, in various colours

needle and pins

tape measure

craft knife

thin bamboo cane

masking tape

1 Pin the silk to a silk-painting frame, pulling the fabric taut. Load a brush with paint, then paint dots of different colours, spacing them approximately 7.5cm/3in apart. Hold the tip of the brush on the silk, and the colours will bleed outwards. Leave the paints to dry naturally.

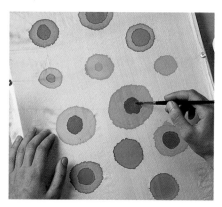

2 Apply a contrast colour dot to the centre of each circle. Allow to dry. Fix (set) the colours with a warm, dry iron. Press and stitch a hem all round. Cut lengths of ribbons and stitch to the corners of the kite.

3 For the strut pockets, cut four pieces of silk, 2cm/¾in square, and press under a seam allowance. Pin a square in each corner on the wrong side and stitch around three sides. Measure the length between the diagonal corners and cut two cane struts to fit. Wrap masking tape around the ends, fit them in the pockets and bind with tape where they cross.

Delicate crêpe de chine, painted with squares of soft colour, makes a beautiful modern room divider. The silk paints make the fabric opaque, so leaving some squares unpainted creates a subtle contrast.

Chequered Screen

you will need

scissors

cream silk crêpe de chine, pre-washed

open-panel screen

old blanket

masking tape

plastic sheet

tailor's chalk pencil

ruler

medium decorator's paintbrush

iron-fix (set) silk paints, in soft colours

iron

sewing machine

matching sewing thread

curtain wire

screw eyes and metal hooks

two pairs of cabinet hinges

1 Cut a panel of silk to fit each frame of the screen, allowing extra for the casings and hems and for the ruched effect. Protect the work surface with a blanket, and tape the plastic over the top. Stretch the first silk panel taut and tape it to the work surface. Using a tailor's chalk pencil and ruler, divide each panel into squares.

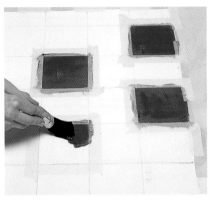

2 Place strips of masking tape around the edges of certain squares. Using a decorator's paintbrush, fill in the squares with the silk paints. Leave some squares unpainted.

3 Leave the paint to dry, then remove the masking tape. Iron the back of the silk, following the manufacturer's instructions, to fix (set) the colours.

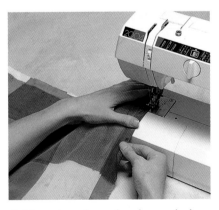

4 Hem the edges of each panel, then make a narrow casing at the top and bottom. Attach lengths of curtain wire to the top and bottom of each frame, using screw eyes and metal hooks. Hinge the screen together, and slip the panels on to the curtain wire.

Paint the background to this flowing design very loosely so that the colours bleed into each other. Leave to dry, then apply wax to protect some areas before adding even richer colours.

Abstract Scarf

you will need

pencil and paper

watercolours or coloured inks

paint palette

artist's paintbrushes

silk pins (push pins)

satin-silk, pre-washed

silk-painting frame

iron-fix (set) silk paints, in 3 colours

large, soft, absorbent paintbrush

batik wax

double boiler or wax pot

household paintbrush

iron

brown craft or lining paper

white spirit (turpentine)

scissors

needle

matching sewing thread

1 Plan your design on paper. It is not necessary to draw it to scale, but it may help to do so. Colour it in, using watercolours or coloured inks, which behave in a similar way to transparent silk paints.

2 Using silk pins (push pins), pin the fabric on to the frame. Check that it is taut and free of wrinkles, and that it will not sag during painting.

3 Mix up the paler silk paint colours first, making sure that you have enough of each colour to cover large areas of the scarf. Use the three base colours to mix additional shades.

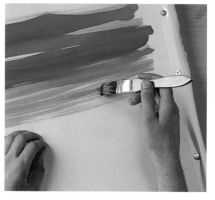

4 You will have to work quite quickly if you want the colours to bleed into each other, so place the plan where you can refer to it easily. Paint the paler areas of the scarf, using a large, soft, absorbent paintbrush and light, flowing movements. Leave to dry.

5 Heat the wax in a double boiler or wax pot to a steady 80°C (170°F). Using a household paintbrush, apply the wax to the areas that will remain pale coloured. The wax should be fully absorbed into the cloth and leave the fabric translucent while it is wet. Leave to dry hard.

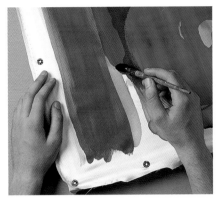

6 Fill in the darker colours, allowing the colours to bleed and overlap each other to create subtle colour blends. Leave the fabric to dry completely.

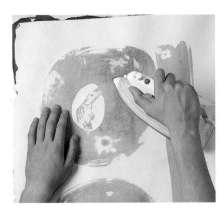

7 Unpin the silk. Remove the wax by placing it between sheets of brown craft or lining paper and ironing over the paper. Fix (set) the paints, using the manufacturer's instructions.

8 Remove any grease marks left on the fabric by soaking it in white spirit (turpentine). Wash the silk several times in warm soapy water to remove the smell. The colours may run slightly, but this will enhance the finished effect. Iron the silk while it is still damp. Trim if necessary so that it is square, then roll the edges and hem stitch by hand.

This beautiful painted and embroidered shawl was inspired by the Indian custom in which a bride's palms are hennaed with intricate designs the night before her wedding.

Indian Motif Shawl

you will need

large heatproof bowl

tablespoon and teaspoon

salt

2 teabags

1m/1yd of 90cm/36in-wide habotai silk, pre-washed

iron

tracing paper and pencil

masking tape

vanishing fabric marker

silk-painting frame

small hammer

dressmaker's pins

gutta applicator

gutta

iron-fix (set) silk paints

palette

medium artist's paintbrush

white paper

embroidery hoop

sewing machine, with a darning foot

machine embroidery threads, in various colours

scissors

needle

1 Fill a bowl with boiling water. Dissolve 60ml/4 tbsp of salt and immerse two teabags in the water. Remove the teabags, then immerse the silk for 10 minutes. Rinse and press the silk using a cool iron.

3 Stretch the fabric over the wooden frame, using a hammer and pins. Ensure that the fabric is taut and that it has no wrinkles. Fill the dispenser with gutta and apply it along the lines of the design. Allow to dry.

5 Leave the paint to dry, then brush away the salt grains. Remove the silk from the frame and place it between two sheets of white paper. Fix (set) the paints, by pressing the silk with an iron following the manufacturer's instructions. Wash the fabric to remove the gutta. Draw star motifs freehand on the background fabric with the fabric marker.

2 Trace the hand template, enlarging as required. Stretch the silk over the template and tape it down. Trace with a vanishing fabric marker. Repeat the design by drawing a grid and rotating the design 90° each time.

4 Pour the silk paints into the palette compartments. Dot a little paint into the centre of each area to be coloured. Apply a wash of colour to the palm then, while the paint is still wet, drop 5ml/1 tsp of salt into the centre.

6 Place the fabric in an embroidery hoop and machine embroider the stars in coloured threads.

7 Using the fabric marker, draw additional circles to overlap the painted ones. Fill in the circles with matching embroidery, working a spiral from the centre to the outline. Stitch two or three lines around the palm area, working small bobbles at intervals. Cut away the excess fabric to within 5cm/2in of the design edge.

◂ **8** Using a needle, carefully pull away the threads around the raw edges to make a fringe.

Hang this silk fabric where it will move gently in the softest breeze. The stylized motifs, drawn freehand, are based on Indian Mogul architectural features such as doors and arched windows.

Double-panelled Room Divider

you will need

tape measure

scissors

4.3m/4¾yd of 115cm/45in-wide medium or heavyweight habotai silk, pre-washed

silk-painting frame

silk pins (push pins)

ruler

vanishing fabric marker

pencil and paper (optional)

gold gutta and applicator

iron-fix (set) silk paints

paint palette

fine and medium artist's paintbrushes

small decorator's paintbrush

iron

needle and matching thread

dressmaker's pins

gold cord

3 small gold tassels

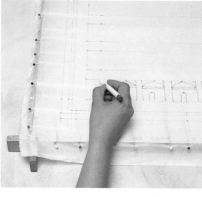

1 Cut two silk panels 115 x 215cm/ 45 x 85in. Stretch the first over the frame, using silk pins. Using a ruler and vanishing fabric marker, draw the borders on the silk, then add the individual motifs. Draw your design on paper first for reference, if you wish.

2 Draw over the lines of the design with gold gutta. Turn over the screen to make sure that the gutta has penetrated through the silk. If there are gaps in the lines, add more gutta to the back of the fabric. Leave to dry.

3 Mix the paint colours, ensuring that you have enough of each. Fill in the solid areas of the design, using artist's paintbrushes. If you dot a little paint in the centre of each area, it will quickly spread as far as the gutta lines.

4 Using a paintbrush, apply diluted washes of colour to fill in the background and borders. Allow to dry and unpin the silk from the frame. Iron to fix (set) the colours. Repeat with the second panel. Stitch the panels together. Pin and slip stitch gold cord around the edge. Stitch the three gold tassels to the bottom corners.

This decorative design is based on a Gothic cathedral window, so rich paint colours are appropriate. Black gutta is used to simulate the effect of the thick leaded lines separating the stained glass.

Stained Glass Panel

you will need

tracing paper and pencil

picture frame

medium-weight silk, pre-washed

masking tape

silk pins (push pins)

silk-painting frame

flat artist's paintbrushes

black gutta

small bowls

iron

iron-fix (set) silk paints, in various

deep colours

thickener

screw-top jar with lid

staple gun

1 Enlarge the template at the back of the book to fit inside the picture frame. Trace it on to the silk, then cover the areas between the lines with masking tape. Using silk pins, pin the silk to a silk-painting frame, pulling the fabric taut.

2 Using a flat artist's paintbrush, fill in the lines between the masking tape with black gutta. Leave the gutta to dry, then apply further coats to make solid lines. Leave to dry. Remove the tape, then take the silk off the frame. Set (fix) the gutta by ironing on the reverse side of the silk.

3 Pin the silk to the painting frame again. Fill in the spaces between the black gutta lines, using coloured silk paints. Leave to dry.

4 In order to paint in more detail, mix thickener into one of the darker colours by placing both in a jar and shaking vigorously. The thickened paint will give a textured brush effect.

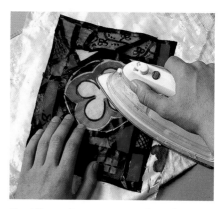

5 Allow the paints to dry, then fix them with an iron, following the manufacturer's instructions. Remove the back from the picture frame. Mount the silk by stretching it over the backless frame, and then secure it at the back using a staple gun.

Dye a length of crêpe de chine in your chosen colour, then use a fine paintbrush and bleach to remove some of the dye. Wash the bleach out immediately to prevent the fabric from rotting.

Spotted Sarong

you will need

scissors

tape measure

silk crêpe de chine, pre-washed

powder dye

vanishing fabric marker

circular objects, to use as templates

silk pins (push pins)

silk-painting frame

bleach

small bowl

fine artist's paintbrush

needle

matching sewing thread

1 Cut a piece of crêpe de chine 150 x 120cm/60 x 48in. Dampen the fabric and then dye it. Using a vanishing fabric marker, draw a grid on the silk. Draw a circular design on to the fabric, using the grid and circular objects to outline the shapes.

2 Pin the fabric taut on to a frame. Pour a little bleach into a bowl. Using a paintbrush, apply dots of bleach to the design, adding it a little at a time to lighten the fabric. Wash the fabric immediately to remove the bleach and leave to dry.

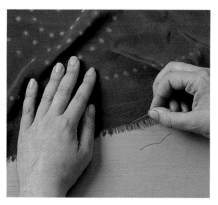

3 To make a narrow fringe along one short edge, carefully separate and remove horizontal threads using a needle. Finish the other three sides by rolling the edges and hem stitching them neatly in place.

If you are a confident artist, you can draw this lovely design directly on to silk without the aid of a paper pattern or template. Use a ruler and different-sized plates to help you mark out the shapes if not.

Zodiac Scarf

you will need

silk pins (push pins)

silk square, pre-washed and hemmed

silk-painting frame

vanishing fabric marker

paper, tracing paper and pencil (optional)

transparent gutta and applicator

iron-fix (set) silk paints

fine artist's paintbrushes

iron

1 Stretch and pin the silk on to the frame. Draw a geometric design on to the silk, using a vanishing fabric marker. Alternatively, draw a design on paper and trace it on to the silk.

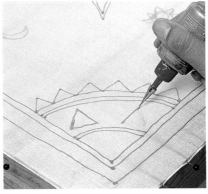

2 Apply the gutta over the drawn lines. It is important for the gutta line to be solid, to prevent the paint from bleeding, so check for any gaps. Leave to dry.

3 After the gutta has dried, apply the silk paints. Leave to dry. Carefully remove the silk from the frame and iron to fix (set) the paints, following the manufacturer's instructions. Hand wash to remove the gutta.

This vibrant picture uses transparent gutta to control the paints. Build up the design by overpainting, using the darkest colours last. Experiment with overpainting your choice of colours before you start.

Poppy Painting

1 Enlarge the template from the back of the book to the size of the finished painting. Pin the silk to the frame and trace the design on to the silk.

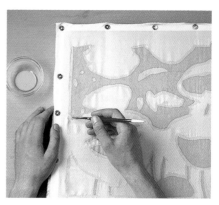

2 Apply transparent gutta around the areas where the palest colours will be. Fill in the palest colour, in this case a yellow which will be over-painted to create shades of green and orange-red. Fix (set) the paint, using an iron. Remove the painting from the frame and rinse away the gutta lines.

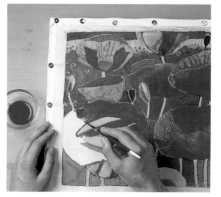

3 Build up the design, keeping the darkest colours until last.

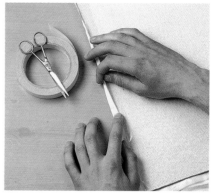

4 Cut a piece of backing to the size of the picture. Put a tiny piece of double-sided tape in each corner of the backing and position the silk on top. Turn the backing over and run double-sided tape along each edge, then pull the fabric round the edge and stick it down. Frame your work.

Use a very fine silk such as chiffon or georgette for this beautiful, flowing design, which you can make to any size. The thickened paints can be applied with a sponge.

Stencilled Lily Scarf

you will need

tracing paper and pencil

acetate sheet

black marker pen

craft knife and cutting mat

chiffon or georgette, pre-washed

silk pins (push pins)

silk-painting frame

iron-fix (set) silk paints, in 3 colours

wide, soft artist's paintbrush

iron

board and backing cloth

masking tape

tailor's chalk

thickener

screw-top jar with lid

sponge

1 Enlarge the template from the back of the book and trace it on to acetate using a marker pen. Cut around the design and cut out the spots using a craft knife. Stretch and pin the fabric to the frame, pulling it taut as you pin.

2 Apply paint to the fabric in random brushstrokes, allowing each colour to dry before applying the next. Remove from the frame and press the silk. Stretch the silk over a board covered with a cloth and tape down.

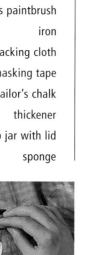

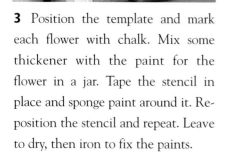

3 Position the template and mark each flower with chalk. Mix some thickener with the paint for the flower in a jar. Tape the stencil in place and sponge paint around it. Reposition the stencil and repeat. Leave to dry, then iron to fix the paints.

This spectacular design is painted on silk-satin. The first vibrant colours are allowed to flow into each other and left to dry, then the red petal outlines are added with a fine paintbrush.

Sunflower Cushion Cover

you will need

white silk-satin, 2½ times the size of
the cushion pad, plus a
1.5cm/⅝in seam allowance
tailor's chalk
silk pins (push pins)
silk-painting frame
iron-fix (set) silk paints, in yellow, red,
blue, turquoise and ultramarine
paint-mixing container
large flat-bristled paintbrush
medium and fine artist's paintbrushes
iron
sewing machine and silk thread
needle

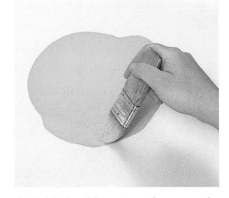

1 Fold the fabric into three panels, two the size of the cushion pad and one half the size (to form the flap). Mark the panels with chalk. Centre the middle panel on the frame. Brush yellow paint from the centre outwards, using a large flat brush.

2 Before the paint dries, add red paint to the yellow to make orange and redefine the centre of the circle. Add blue to the paint to make green and make a smaller circle in the centre of the orange. Add dots in the centre with more blue paint. Leave to dry.

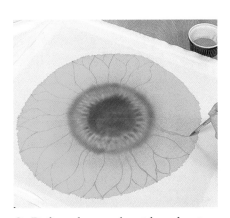

3 Define the petals with red paint. Fill in the background with shades of blue. Fix the paint. Press under and stitch a double hem on each short edge. Fold right sides together, so that the flap covers half the front. Fold the back over both, then stitch the side seams. Turn through, insert a cushion pad and stitch the gap.

Batik

Traditional batik is known for its delicate patterns of vein-like lines, created by applying hot wax to the surface of the fabric and then cracking the wax when it is cold so that coloured dyes can seep in. The technique of wax resist can be used to create designs large and small, including napkins, room dividers and beautiful silk and velvet scarves.

Wax, Crackle and Paint

Traditional batik dyeing has a very long history, dating back over 2,000 years. The word "batik" is Indonesian, and batik is most commonly associated with the Indonesian island of Java.

The batik technique works on the principle that wax acts as a barrier, or "resist", to water and therefore also to diluted dyes.

The wax has to be heated to the correct temperature before being applied to the fabric surface, and it is important to maintain a constant temperature, so a thermometer is essential. The wax should make the fabric semi-transparent when it is applied; if the fabric remains opaque, the wax isn't hot enough. If in doubt, test a spare piece of fabric before embarking on the final piece.

Various brushes and tools (even a piece of string) can be used to apply the

wax, but the traditional Indonesian "tjanting" allows very precise and delicate patterns to be drawn in the same way as a pen. It takes a little practice to master the flow of the hot wax through the tjanting so that it comes out evenly in a

continuous, unbroken line. As the wax cools, it becomes brittle and can be gently cracked by rubbing the fabric between your hands. When the waxed fabric is immersed in a dye bath the colour seeps into the cracks, creating a random, unpredictable and unique colour pattern. The more cracks you make, the more the dye will penetrate the fabric. Further layers of wax and dye can be applied to the cleaned fabric to build up a complex design, although striking, contemporary effects can be achieved quite simply using just one or two vibrant colours.

In a quite different version of batik – known as the direct dyeing method and as "false batik" – the fabric is not dyed in a dye bath but is painted using iron-fix (set) silk paints or fabric paints.

Whichever method you choose, traditional and modern batik designs work very successfully on a wide range of smooth, natural fabrics, including cotton, silk and even leather.

The most important materials used in batik are the wax for the resist, the double boiler to heat the wax, and the dyes or paints to colour the fabric, depending on which technique you are using.

Materials

wax and dyes to penetrate the fibres. Cotton can be boiled, but silk should be dry-cleaned to remove the wax.

General-purpose batik wax
Available ready-mixed in granular form from craft suppliers, this is the simplest wax for a beginner to use. Different waxes are available to create special effects. Heat and apply the wax following the manufacturer's instructions. Work in a well-ventilated area.

Kitchen paper
Use to blot up excess paint.

Leather
Batik works well on leather, using a clear, water-soluble household glue or gum instead of wax as a resist. Don't use wax on leather as it will stain it. Special dyes and finishing treatments such as leather lacquer spray are available for leather – always follow the manufacturer's instructions.

Newspaper, brown craft or lining paper
Insert waxed fabric between sheets of paper and iron to remove the wax. Replace with new paper until all the wax is removed.

Sponge
Use to make stencils.

Bleach
Colour can be removed from a pre-dyed fabric by placing it in a bowl of diluted bleach. Always wear rubber gloves and work in a well-ventilated area. Rinse fabric with water and vinegar to neutralize the bleach.

Cotton wool (Cotton balls)
Clip a wad of cotton wool into a clothes peg (pin) to make a homemade painting tool for covering large areas.

Dyes and silk paints
Use cold-water dyes, in powder or liquid form. Dyes or silk paints can also be applied in concentrated form. Special dyes are available for working with leather.

Fabrics
Use natural fabrics such as cotton and silk – those without texture are the most suitable. Pre-wash the fabric to remove any dressing, and to allow the

Heating wax for batik requires a wax pot or double boiler, and a thermometer. You will probably also use a dye bath or painting frame, and a traditional tjanting.

Equipment

Chalk

Can be used to lightly trace a design on to dark-coloured fabric.

Craft knife

Use to cut thick paper and cardboard. Work on a cutting mat to protect the work surface.

Dye bath, buckets and bowls

Special shallow dye baths are ideal for batik dyeing. Alternatively, use a metal or plastic catering tray, or a large saucepan, bucket or bowl in which the fabric can move freely. If you are using a hot-water dye, the dye bath must be heatproof. Keep the fabric immersed so that the dye penetrates evenly.

Hairdryer and iron

Use a hairdryer to fix (set) silk dyes that are awkward shapes. Be careful not to melt the wax. Use an iron to remove wax from fabric and to set dye.

Masking tape

Use to attach fabric to a board or work surface to hold it in place.

Paintbrushes

Artist's and decorator's paintbrushes of various sizes can be used. Use a separate brush to apply wax. Use sponge brushes to apply paint over large areas of fabric. Alternatively, use a large kitchen sponge.

Painting frame

Stretch fabric taut over a wooden painting frame before tracing a design on to the fabric surface.

Rubber gloves

Wear rubber gloves when dyeing fabric to avoid staining your hands.

Thermometer

Some wax pots are thermostatically controlled, but, if not, a kitchen thermometer is essential to keep the batik wax at a constant temperature while you are applying it to the fabric.

Tjanting

This traditional pen-like tool is used to draw wax designs on the fabric. Many sizes of nibs (tips) are available.

Wool dauber

A tool used to apply leather dyes.

Good, thorough preparation is the key to success with every fabric painting technique, and will help to ensure that better and more consistent results are achieved.

Techniques

Making a basic wooden painting frame

A wooden frame is essential for batik. Make a basic frame slightly larger than the size of the finished batik piece.

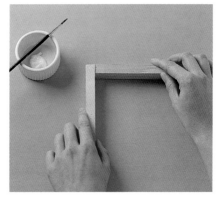

1 Cut four pieces of planed wood to the size you want your frame to be. Using wood adhesive, glue two sets of two pieces together to make right angles. Allow the glue to set.

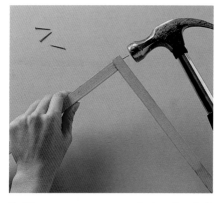

2 Tap one or two panel pins (tacks) into the corner joint to hold it firmly. Glue the right angles together to make the frame and nail the corners as before.

3 Sand down any rough pieces of wood so that it is free of splinters. Protect the frame from dye by covering it with masking tape.

Pinning fabric over the frame

Special assa pins (push pins) with three prongs are available from craft suppliers, for fixing fabric to the wooden frame.

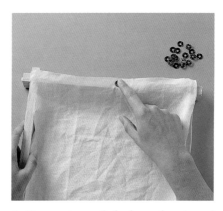

1 Cut a piece of cloth to the size of the frame and place the first push pin in the centre of the furthest edge.

2 Working out towards each corner, continue placing the pins an equal distance apart. Pull the fabric taut.

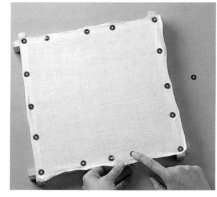

3 Pull the fabric across the frame, and place the pins opposite to those on the first side. Pull the fabric taut. Repeat on the other two sides.

Traditional batik   Traditional batik is best used when large areas of colour are required. When using a dye bath, use a cold-water dye so the consistency of the wax is not affected, and keep the cloth flat while submerged in dye.

1 Place the batik wax in a wax pot or double boiler and gently heat it to a steady 80°C (170°F). Apply melted wax along the outline of the design, using a tjanting or other instrument such as a paintbrush or cotton wool. The wax should leave a transparent line on the fabric. If the wax is not hot enough, it will sit on the surface of the fabric without penetrating the fibres sufficiently. Leave the wax to dry.

2 Mix up a dye bath with a cold water dye, following the dye manufacturer's instructions. Remove the cloth from the frame. Dampen it and place it in the dye bath, keeping the waxed area as flat as possible. When the desired colour has been achieved, remove the fabric from the bath and rinse it in cold water. Unless cracking is required, be careful not to crease the fabric while rinsing. Hang it up to dry.

3 When the cloth is dry, re-pin it on to the frame, pulling it taut, and fill in any areas with wax that you want to remain the colour of the first dye. Check the back to make sure that the wax has penetrated sufficiently. Prepare a second dye bath. Add the fabric to it, being careful not to fold the waxed areas. After dyeing, rinse it thoroughly in cold water. Hang up to dry through.

4 Remove the wax by ironing the cloth between pieces of newspaper, brown paper or lining paper.

5 Wax and dye can be added to build up more layers of colour and detail. However, most dyes can only be overlaid about three times.

False method or direct dyeing

This principle uses wax as a boundary, where one colour is separated from another by a line of wax. It is imperative that the lines of wax have no breaks, or the colours will bleed into each other.

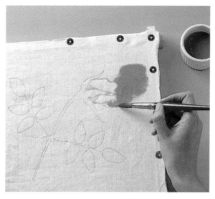

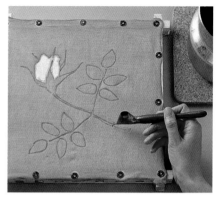

1 Pin the fabric to the frame, transfer the design and heat the wax as for the traditional batik method. Using a tjanting, draw in any outlines with wax. When the wax is applied, the fabric should become semi-transparent. If the wax has not penetrated the fibres sufficiently, the fabric will remain opaque. Check for breaks in the wax outline and fill them in by waxing on the back.

2 Using fabric dye (transparent dyes not containing binders, such as silk paints, are ideal), fill in the required areas with a paintbrush. Work quickly to ensure an even colour. If you choose to use a thick fabric paint, be sure to dilute it to the consistency of ink.

3 Draw in more of the outline with molten wax and tjanting. Check the back of the fabric again to make sure that the wax has penetrated the fibres of the fabric sufficiently.

4 Using a different colour, fill in the background with a paintbrush. Further applications of dye can be made on the remaining non-waxed areas.

5 Apply a third colour. Waxing and dyeing can continue indefinitely or until the whole cloth is covered. To remove the wax, see Finishing.

Special treatments Although the tjanting is the traditional tool used for applying wax, other tools such as paintbrushes and cotton wool pads can be used to achieve different effects. Once complete, take time to finish the work methodically.

Tjanting

The tjanting allows delicate designs to be drawn on to fabric with wax. Keep movements light and do not press on the fabric too hard as this may block the flow of wax.

Cracking

Here the fabric was coated in a layer of wax. It was crumpled, to crack the wax surface. Dye the fabric in a dye bath for best results and use a brittle crackle wax.

Decorator's paintbrush

This cross-hatching effect was made using a medium-sized decorator's paintbrush. Lightly draw the waxed brush across the undyed fabric horizontally and then vertically.

Finishing Wax must be removed from the finished batik to restore the fabric's drape. Ironing will remove most of the wax, but it will be necessary to boil or dry-clean the fabric to remove final marks and wax residue.

1 Break away as much of the hardened wax as you can. Do not scrub the fabric as this may damage the surface.

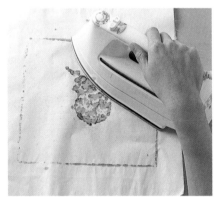

2 Place the batik between sheets of newspaper, brown or lining paper, and iron until the wax is absorbed. Repeat until wax is no longer being absorbed.

3 To use the boiling method, break off as much wax as possible then place the fabric in boiling water for about 10 minutes, stirring continuously.

Use this lovely screen as a room divider, or place it in front of a window or lamp where the light will shine through the delicate silk fabric. Various brushes and techniques give added interest.

Lightweight Folding Screen

you will need

tape measure

folding wooden screen

scissors

lightweight silk, pre-washed

silk pins (push pins)

silk-painting frame

heat-fixed (set) dyes, in lilac, lime green and pale blue

sponge brush

hairdryer

general-purpose wax

wax pot or double boiler

tjanting

medium artist's paintbrush

coarse decorator's paintbrush

salt

iron

newspaper, brown or lining paper

narrow double-sided tape

staple gun

masking tape

strong fabric glue

ribbon or braid

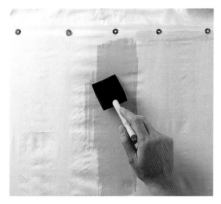

1 Measure the inside edge of each panel of the screen and add at least 3cm/1¼in wastage all round. Cut the silk to size. Pin the first panel to the painting frame. Divide the length roughly in half between lilac and lime green, then apply these dyes quickly using a sponge brush and allowing the paints to blend together in the middle. Dry the silk with a hairdryer to fix (set) the dyes.

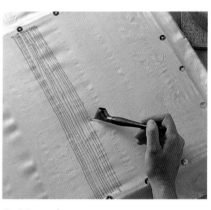

2 Heat the wax in a wax pot or a double boiler (see Techniques). In the top quarter of the silk, draw fine lines of wax freehand with a tjanting. Drawing the lines freehand will add spontaneity to the design.

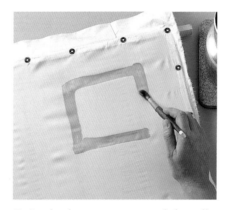

3 In the bottom quarter of the silk, draw a square of wax using a medium artist's paintbrush. You can experiment with other brushes and tools to create a variety of marks.

4 Using a coarse decorator's paintbrush, overpaint the entire panel in pale blue. Leave to dry. Paint a stripe of wax down one side of the panel.

5 Overpaint the panel again and leave to dry. Add more stripes or squares as desired. Sprinkle salt on the damp dye in some places to create an interesting textured effect. Leave to dry completely before brushing off the salt grains.

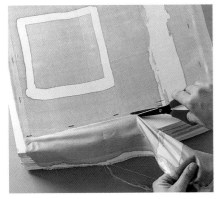

7 Stretch one of the panels across the frame, sticking it to the double-sided tape. Pull the silk tight, making sure there are no wrinkles and that the cloth is springy to the touch. The silk can be pulled up from the tape and re-stuck if adjustments are needed.

Staple the edges of the cloth even-ly to the frame. Trim away any cloth that is unstuck using a pair of sharp scissors. Cover the raw edges with masking tape to prevent fraying. Using strong fabric glue, cover the untidy topside edges with ribbon or braid. Repeat to cover all the remain-ing frames that make up the screen.

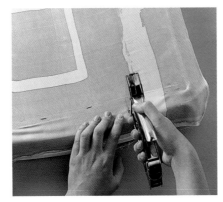

6 Remove the silk panel from the frame. Remove the wax by ironing the silk between sheets of newspaper, brown or lining paper. Prepare the remaining panels for each frame of the screen. On the first panel, run a strip of narrow double-sided tape around the inside edge of the frame (on the face of the screen).

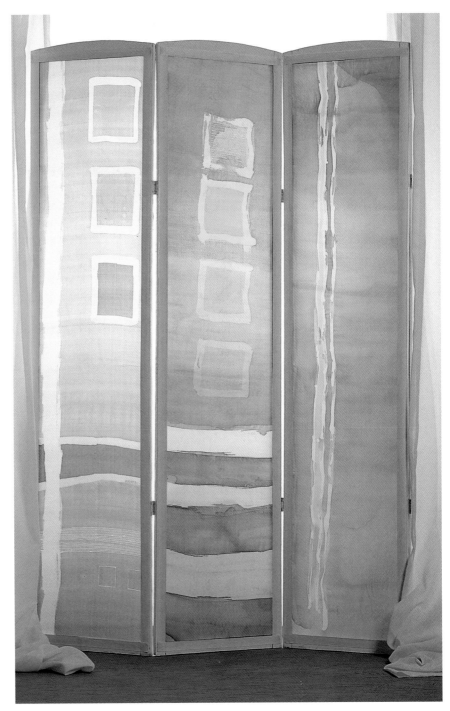

This simple design of squares within squares is drawn freehand on a measured grid to give a spontaneous look. The two-tone background fabric adds extra interest.

Vibrant Silk Cushion Cover

you will need

pencil, ruler and set square (t-square)

two-tone dupion silk, pre-washed

vanishing fabric marker

silk pins (push pins)

silk-painting frame

general-purpose wax

wax pot or double boiler

tjanting

iron-fix (set) silk paints

paintbrushes

iron

newspaper, brown or lining paper

scissors

dressmaker's pins

sewing machine

matching sewing thread

40cm/16in-square cushion pad

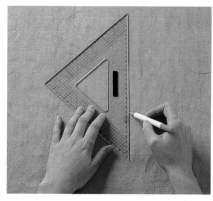

1 Mark a 42cm/17in square on the silk with a pencil. Mark out a grid in the centre using a vanishing fabric marker. The grid should be three squares across and three squares down, each square measuring 10cm/4in.

2 Pin the silk taut to a painting frame. It should be springy to the touch. Heat the wax in a wax pot or double boiler (see Techniques). Wax in the grid using a tjanting. It is important that there are no breaks in the outline so check the back for areas of fabric that remain opaque once the wax has been applied. Fill in any breaks with wax on the back.

3 Fill in the grid with diluted silk paints. Allow the paints to blend out from the brush to the wax outline rather than overloading the fabric with dye, as this may cause the colour to bleed underneath the wax.

4 Leave to dry, then draw in the remainder of the design, squares within squares. Do not use a ruler for this – it will add to the effect if the squares are slightly irregular. Wax over the design lines.

5 Check the back for breaks in the outline and fill them with wax. Fill in the remaining colours using deep reds, purples, olive and brown. Use a different brush for each colour.

6 Remove the silk from the frame and iron out the wax between sheets of newspaper, brown or lining paper. To remove any remaining grease marks, have the finished cover dry-cleaned. Trim the fabric down to the marked 42cm/17in square.

7 Cut two pieces of silk 42 x 28cm/ 17 x 11in for the back. Stitch a double 1cm/½in hem along one long edge of each. Place the batik square right side up. Pin the two rectangles on top, face down, with the hemmed edges in the centre.

8 Stitch all the way round the cover, leaving a 1cm/½in seam allowance. Stitch a line of zigzag stitches between the sewn seam and the raw edge to prevent fraying. Turn the cover right side out and insert the cushion pad.

Decorate a ready made cotton napkin (or set of matching napkins) with this stylish design. Use colourfast dyes that will withstand repeated machine washing.

Geometric Napkin

you will need

ruler

pencil and tracing paper

white cotton napkin, pre-washed

silk pins (push pins)

painting frame

vanishing fabric marker (optional)

general-purpose wax

wax pot or double boiler

tjanting

colourfast fabric dyes, in pale blue, lilac and cobalt blue

medium artist's spongebrush

iron

newspaper, brown or lining paper

1 Draw a 10cm/4in cross in the centre of the napkin. Pin the napkin to the frame so that it is stretched taut. Draw a grid on tracing paper to fit the 10cm/4in cross. Turn the frame upside down over the design, lining up the central crosses. Trace the design on to the fabric, using a pen that will show through the fabric.

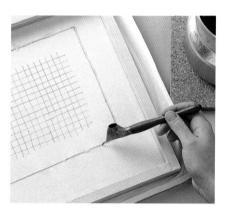

2 Heat the wax in a wax pot or a double boiler (see Techniques). Draw in the main square with wax, using a tjanting. There should be no breaks in the wax outline and the cloth should appear semi-transparent. Check the back for areas of the cloth that remain opaque, and reapply the molten wax to the back.

3 Using an artist's spongebrush, fill in the central square with pale blue dye. Do not overload the cloth or the colour may bleed into the white border. Allow the dye to bleed out from the brush, especially when working near the wax outline. Leave to dry.

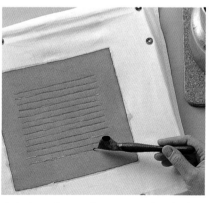

4 When the napkin is completely dry, wax in all the horizontal lines using the tjanting. Paint the central square with lilac dye. Once again, do not overload the fabric with dye.

5 Leave to dry, then wax in all the vertical lines. Fill in the central square with cobalt blue. Remove the napkin from the frame. Place the napkin between sheets of newspaper, brown or lining paper and iron to remove the wax. Dry-clean the fabric.

Decorate a plain silk tie with a simple design of stripes and dots. Use a piece of waxed string to mark out the stripes and a traditional tjanting to apply the dots.

Striped Silk Tie

you will need

general-purpose wax

wax pot or double boiler

white silk tie, pre-washed

plastic board

string

medium-spout tjanting

iron-fix (set) silk paints, in pale blue and dark blue

medium decorator's paintbrush or sponge brush

kitchen paper

brush (for wax)

iron

newspaper, brown or lining paper

1 Heat the wax in a wax pot or a double boiler (see Techniques). Place the tie flat on a plastic board. Put a piece of string in the wax, and wait for the melted wax to coat the string. Pull it taut, then apply the wax across the tie to create a striped pattern.

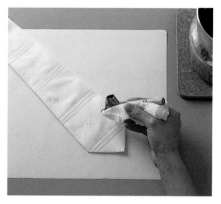

2 Using a tjanting, add dots of wax between the stripes.

3 Cover the tie with pale blue silk paint. Turn over the tie and paint on the back. Blot with kitchen paper to absorb any excess dye. Leave to dry.

4 Apply more wax with a brush across the white spots.

5 Repeat step 3 with dark blue paint. Iron the tie between sheets of paper. Continue ironing between clean sheets of paper until no more wax appears. The heat will also fix (set) the paint. Have the tie dry-cleaned to remove the excess wax.

A cheerful cup design decorates this simple cotton table mat. It is padded with a layer of wadding (batting), then hand quilted to absorb heat and protect your tabletop.

Quilted Table Mat

you will need

silk pins (push pins)

lightweight white cotton, pre-washed

painting frame

tracing paper

vanishing fabric marker

general-purpose wax

wax pot or double boiler

tjanting

medium artist's paintbrush

colourfast dyes, in sky blue, yellow, etc

iron

newspaper, brown or lining paper

scissors

medium-thickness wadding (batting)

needle

tacking (basting) thread

bias binding

dressmaker's pins

sewing machine

matching sewing thread

embroidery thread (floss)

embroidery needle

1 Pin the cotton on to the painting frame. Enlarge the template from the back of the book. Turn the frame upside down over the design and trace with a vanishing fabric marker. If the design is not visible, trace the design on to the surface of the cloth using tracing paper.

2 Heat the wax in a wax pot or a double boiler (see Techniques). Using a tjanting, wax the outlines of the cups. You could also wax a line around the edge of the cloth to keep your work neat. Check the back of the fabric to make sure that the wax has penetrated through.

3 Using a medium artist's paintbrush, fill in the background to the cups with sky blue dye. Fill in the cup shapes with yellow dye. Do not overload the cloth with dye, as it might bleed under the wax barrier. Allow the dyes to bleed out from the brush.

4 Draw the pattern on the cups using a vanishing fabric marker. Wax in the details using the tjanting. Check the back of the fabric for breaks in the wax outline and, if necessary, reapply molten wax to the back.

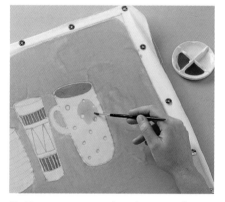

5 Paint in more details, considering how one colour will affect another. Remove the batik from the frame and iron out as much wax as possible between sheets of paper. Any wax residue can be removed from cotton by boiling (see Techniques).

  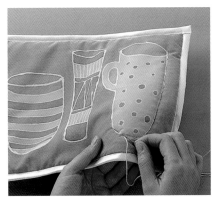

6 Trim the batik to the finished size. Cut a piece of wadding (batting) and a piece of backing the same size. Tack (baste) the three pieces together. Cut a length of bias binding and open out. Align the raw edge of the backing with one edge of the binding. Pin in place. Stitch down the edge of the mat, in the crease.

7 Repeat on the opposite side. Fold the binding to the right side of the mat and top stitch, close to the edge of the binding. Trim the top and bottom of the binding square with the top and bottom of the mat. Repeat on the remaining two sides of the mat, folding the ends in before stitching to give neat corners.

8 Using two or three strands of cotton embroidery thread (floss), work running stitch around the cups, stitching through all the thicknesses of the mat to produce a quilted effect.

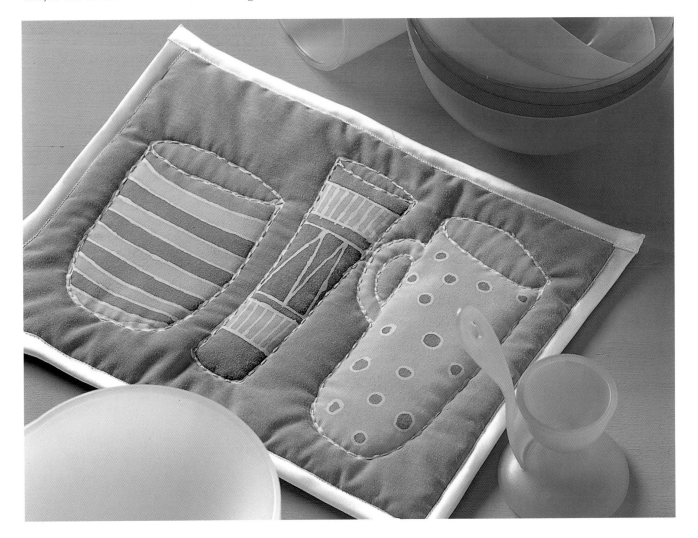

A wax grid forms the base of this simple design, painted in muted lilac and blue colours. Crêpe de chine is used here but any lightweight silk would be equally suitable.

Square Silk Scarf

you will need

tracing paper and pencil

silk pins (push pins)

90cm/36in-square of crêpe de chine silk, pre-washed

silk-painting frame

general-purpose wax

wax pot or double boiler

medium-spout tjanting

sponge brush

iron-fix (set) silk paints, in light blue, royal blue, lilac, purple and dark blue

small bowls

brush (for wax)

kitchen paper

iron

newspaper, brown or lining paper

needle

matching sewing thread

1 Trace and enlarge the template provided. Pin the silk scarf to the frame. Turn frame side up. Place the design right side up under the corner of the silk, 7cm/3in from each side. Using a pencil, trace the design on to the back of the silk. To make the whole design, reverse the template so that the wider corner is at the outer edge. Repeat so that the wide border is around the edge of the scarf.

2 Heat the wax in a wax pot or a double boiler (see Techniques). Apply the wax in spirals on the fabric using a tjanting. Keep your movements light. Make sure that the exterior of the tjanting is free of molten wax as this may smudge on to the scarf.

3 Using a sponge brush, apply light blue silk paint over the whole scarf. Allow the paint to bleed from the brush rather than overloading the fabric. Leave to dry.

4 Using a brush, apply the wax in a grid design.

5 Paint the blue, lilac and purple paint in the squares. Leave to dry.

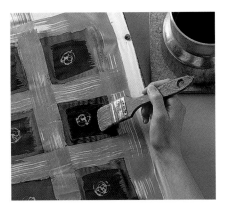

7 Apply dark blue paint over the whole scarf. Blot any excess paint with kitchen paper. Leave to dry. Iron the scarf between sheets of newspaper, brown or lining paper. The heat will also fix (set) the silk paints. Keep changing the paper until no more wax appears. Have the scarf dry-cleaned to remove the excess wax. Roll the edges of the scarf and hand stitch.

6 Cover the coloured areas of the design with wax brushstrokes.

Use simple sponge shapes to create an alternating design of evenly spaced circles and stars on this lovely sarong. Areas of plain colour make an effective contrast to the batik.

Cotton Sarong

you will need

tracing paper and pencil

scissors

masking tape

sponge

felt-tipped pen

craft knife

150cm/60in of 90cm/36in-wide

thin cotton, pre-washed

plastic board or surface

general-purpose wax

wax pot or double boiler

large decorator's brush

large bowls

rubber gloves

dyes, in yellow and dark green

iron

newspaper, brown or lining paper

sewing machine

matching sewing thread

1 Trace the templates at the back of the book. Cut them out and attach to a sponge, using masking tape. Draw around each template. With a craft knife, cut out the sponge shapes.

2 Pin one end of the cotton fabric on to a plastic board. Heat the wax in a wax pot or double boiler (see Techniques) and apply with a large brush around the edge of the sarong.

3 Using the circular sponge, apply the wax, leaving approximately 8cm/3in between each circle. Repeat the pattern around the edge of the border.

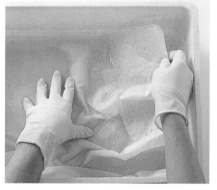

4 Wet the fabric thoroughly. Dye the wet fabric yellow, following the manufacturer's instructions. Hang it up to dry. Pin the fabric back on to the plastic board. Using the same brush, re-wax the border to keep the yellow crackle effect. Wax over the circles again, using the same sponge stencil. Using the cross stencil, apply the wax between the circles.

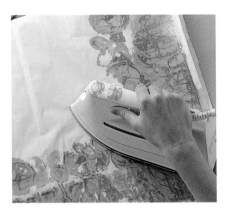

5 Put the fabric in a bowl of water, then dye the wet fabric dark green, following the manufacturer's instructions. Hang it up to dry.

6 Iron the fabric between sheets of paper, until no more wax appears through the paper. Dry-clean the fabric to remove the excess wax. Turn in the raw edges and stitch in place.

Decorate either end of a plain habotai silk scarf with stripes of colour. Seal off the end of each stripe with the wax so that the colours cannot bleed into each other.

Bordered Scarf

you will need

tracing paper, soft pencil, felt-tipped pen, ruler or set square (t-square)

silk pins (push pins)

lightweight habotai silk, pre-washed

silk-painting frame

general-purpose wax

wax pot or double boiler

tjanting

iron-fix (set) silk paints

paint palette

fine artist's paintbrush

hairdryer

iron

newspaper, brown or lining paper

scissors and needle

matching sewing thread

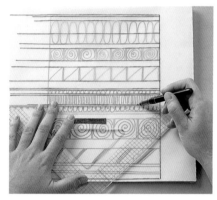

1 Enlarge the design provided at the back of the book. Trace off the horizontal lines. Pin one end of the silk to the frame. Choose a frame that is slightly deeper than the height of the border design, remembering to allow for wastage all round.

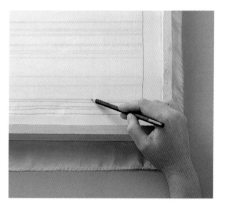

2 Turn the frame upside down on to the design and trace off all the horizontal lines, using a soft pencil. Heat the wax (see Techniques). Wax the horizontal stripes using a tjanting. Close in the ends of each stripe to prevent the paints from bleeding. The waxed lines should be semi-transparent. Wax any that aren't on the back.

3 Fill in the stripes with pale colours, such as smoky blue, terracotta or pale pink. Leave to dry. Fix (set) the silk paints using a hairdryer; be careful not to melt the wax.

4 Replace the frame upside down on the design and trace off the detail and patterning. Wax in these details with the tjanting.

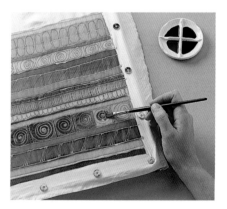

5 Paint over the stripes and details with darker colours, such as purple, blue, deep red and brown. Remove some of the hardened wax with your fingers. Repeat the process for the opposite end of the scarf.

6 Iron the batik between sheets of paper to remove the wax. The fabric will still be stiff at this stage. Trim off the wastage. If possible, tear the silk to ensure a straight edge. Roll the edges of the scarf and hand stitch. Dry-clean the finished scarf to restore the drape and sheen of the silk.

This rich autumnal table runner is coloured with both paints and dyes in rich dark tones. Position the leaves at different angles to give the design a natural look.

Maple Leaf Table Runner

you will need

scissors and tape measure

dupion silk, pre-washed

tracing paper and pencil

Mylar film

craft knife and cutting mat

silk pins (push pins)

silk-painting frame

vanishing fabric marker

crackle or general-purpose wax

wax pot or double boiler

tjanting

brush (for wax)

fine artist's paintbrushes

direct-application dyes, in rusty brown and olive green

brown dye

dye bath

iron

newspaper, brown or lining paper

needle

matching sewing thread

scissors

1 Cut a piece of dupion silk to the required size, adding a 2cm/¾in seam allowance all round and 2–4cm/¾–1½in wastage. Trace the maple leaf from the back of the book, and cut out of Mylar film using a craft knife.

2 Pin the silk to the painting frame. Using the template and a vanishing fabric marker, draw maple leaves randomly over the cloth. Place the leaves at different angles so that they look scattered rather than neatly placed.

3 Heat the wax in a wax pot or a double boiler (see Techniques). Using a tjanting, apply wax around the outline of some of the leaves. Block in the remaining leaves with a brush. Check the back of the fabric for breaks in the wax outline, and fill in any gaps by waxing on the back.

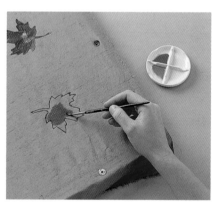

4 Using a small artist's paintbrush, paint in the leaves that have a wax outline with dyes. Use rusty brown and olive green colours. Leave to dry.

5 Block in the painted leaves with wax. All the leaves should now be solidly waxed. Remove the fabric from the frame and crumple it in your hands to crack the surface of the wax.

6 Wet the batik and place it in a dark brown dye bath following the manufacturer's instructions. When the cloth is the desired colour, rinse it thoroughly. Leave to dry.

7 Iron the fabric between two sheets of paper until wax is no longer being absorbed. Have the fabric dry-cleaned to remove any wax residue.

8 Using a needle, remove individual threads from opposite ends of the runner to make a fringe. Press a 1cm/½in double hem on the two remaining sides. Hem stitch each hem in place by hand. Divide the fringe at the top and bottom into equal sections and knot threads together. Trim the ends of the tassels evenly.

Batik on silk velvet creates a lovely mottled effect. Use a sponge to help the wax penetrate the thick pile of the velvet, and apply at least two layers of wax over each area to protect the fabric.

Silk Velvet Scarf

you will need

tracing paper and pencil

scissors

felt-tipped pen

sponge

craft knife

silk pins (push pins) or masking tape

130 x 27cm/52 x 10½in of

white silk velvet

plastic board or surface

general-purpose wax

wax pot or double boiler

large bowls

rubber gloves

bucket

dyes, in gold and dark brown

newspaper

iron

brown or lining paper (optional)

knife

sewing machine

matching sewing thread

needle

1 Trace the diamond template at the back of the book. Cut it out and draw around it on to a piece of sponge. Cut out the shape with a craft knife.

2 Pin or tape one end of the silk velvet on to a plastic board or surface.

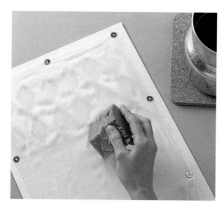

3 Heat the wax in a wax pot or a double boiler (see Techniques). Apply it in three rows, using the diamond-shaped sponge stencil. Apply single diamonds randomly along the scarf length. Re-attach the scarf at the other end and repeat the design. Repeat the process to protect the velvet. Unpin the fabric.

4 Place the velvet in a bowl of water. Wearing rubber gloves, put the wet fabric in a bucket of gold dye, agitate and remove after approximately 3 minutes. Blot between sheets of newspaper to remove excess dye, then hang up to dry.

5 Pin the fabric to the plastic board. Wax the gold areas using the sponge stencil, then repeat the waxing to protect the gold velvet. Roughly wax over the white diamonds again, to keep the gold crackle effect. Remove the fabric from the board.

◀ **6** Wet the fabric, then dye it dark brown and agitate for a few minutes. Blot between sheets of paper and hang up to dry. Iron the velvet between sheets of newsprint, pile side down. When the wax is softened, scrape it off the pile with a knife. Turn the velvet over again and keep ironing until most of the wax has been absorbed by the paper. Remove the excess wax by dry cleaning. Stitch the fabric together lengthwise, with right sides facing. Leave an 8cm/3in-gap along the side and turn the scarf right side out. Hand sew the gap. Steam the seams flat.

The marbled effect on this fabric was created using the "crackle" technique. Some of the wax is deliberately left in the fabric to make it water-resistant, and the bag also has a practical nylon lining.

Crackle-finish Cosmetic Bag

you will need

scissors

medium-weight cotton fabric, pre-washed

silk pins (push pins)

wooden painting frame

crackle or general-purpose wax

wax pot or double boiler

medium decorator's paintbrush

dye bath

dyes, in navy blue and green

hairdryer

iron

newspaper, brown or lining paper

waterproof nylon fabric

dressmaker's pins

sewing machine

matching sewing thread

needle

bias binding

ribbon or cord

1 Cut a piece of cotton fabric the size required for the finished washbag, adding 1cm/½in seam allowance all round. Using silk pins (push pins), pin the fabric on to a wooden painting frame. Heat the wax in a wax pot or double boiler (see Techniques), then cover the entire fabric with wax using a medium decorator's paintbrush.

2 Once the wax has set, remove the fabric from the frame and crumple it firmly between both hands. Small cracks should appear in the surface of the wax. Once the fabric has been "cracked" enough, smooth it out flat and dampen.

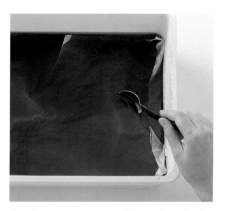

3 Prepare a navy blue dye bath, following the manufacturer's instructions. Place the damp fabric in the bath for the recommended time, allowing the dye to penetrate the cracks in the wax.

4 Rinse the fabric in cold water until the water runs clear. Leave to dry. Re-pin the fabric on to the painting frame. Heat the wax with a hairdryer until it melts, so that the molten wax seals up the cracks.

5 When the wax has set, crumple the fabric again between your hands. Repeat step 3, using a strong green dye. Rinse the batik until the water runs clear, then remove as much wax as possible with your fingers.

6 Iron out more of the wax by placing the batik between pieces of newspaper, brown or lining paper. Keep renewing the paper and ironing until the fabric has regained most of its flexibility, but still contains some wax.

7 Cut the batik in half then cut two pieces of nylon fabric to the same sizes, for the lining. With right sides together, pin, then machine stitch up one side of the batik, leaving a 1cm/½in gap 1cm/½in from the top. Iron the side seam flat, then oversew around the gap by hand to reinforce it. Stitch the other side seam and across the bottom to make the bag.

8 Take the two pieces of lining and stitch round three sides, using a 1cm/½in seam allowance, to make another bag. Place the batik bag inside the lining bag, with wrong sides together.

9 Open up a piece of bias binding long enough to fit the length of the top of the bag. Align the raw edge of the bag with one long edge of the binding. Pin, then stitch round the edge of the bag, using the crease on the bias binding as a guide for stitching. Turn the bag right side out. Fold the bias binding over to the right side of the bag, and fold the raw edge in. Top stitch the binding to the bag, keeping as close to the folded edge of the binding as possible.

10 Stitch two parallel lines to make a channel round the top of the bag just clearing the top and bottom of the gap in the side seam.

11 Thread ribbon or cord through the hole and along the channel. Pull up to close the bag.

Transform an old canvas deckchair with this wonderfully eye-catching design. Allowing the colours to bleed into each other creates the soft, furry effect of the tiger's stripes.

Tiger Deckchair

you will need

old deckchair

tracing paper and pencil

heavyweight canvas, pre-washed

painting frame

assa (push) pins

wax pot or double boiler

general-purpose wax

tjanting

brushes (for wax)

dyes (for direct dyeing method)

soft brushes (for dye)

large sponge brush or soft

kitchen sponge

hairdryer (optional)

newspaper, brown or lining paper

iron

scissors

dressmaker's pins

sewing machine

matching sewing thread

hammer

upholstery pins

1 Remove the fabric from the deck-chair. Draw around it adding 2cm/¾in all round for seams. Trace the design provided on to the canvas. Continue the stripes until the cloth is covered. Pin the cloth taut to a frame.

2 Heat the wax in a wax pot or a double boiler. Using a tjanting, wax the outline of the tiger's head, paws, eyelashes and irises. If the wax does not penetrate the heavy fabric, fill in the breaks in the wax on the back.

3 Using a tjanting and/or brush, block in the claws and whites of the eyes with wax. Fill in the iris and eye-lashes with dark brown and olive green dyes. Using a larger brush, fill in the background to the tiger (the base of the cloth on the finished chair).

4 Fill in the tiger background colour. Fade the colours from a pale orange at the tiger's head to a strong cherry red at the other end of the fabric. Work quickly so that the colours bleed into each other while still wet. To help with quick coverage, use a large sponge brush or soft kitchen sponge.

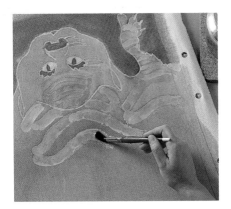 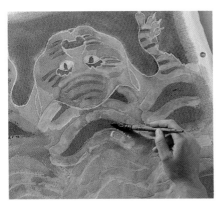 

5 If you are using an iron-fix (set) dye, use a hairdryer to help dry the fabric. When the fabric is dry, use a brush to wax the outline to the tiger stripes. Use a thicker brush when you are about halfway down the fabric.

6 Paint the stripes with dark brown. Remove the batik from the frame and pick off as much wax as possible. Place the cloth between sheets of newspaper, brown or lining paper and iron. To remove final remnants of wax, have the batik dry-cleaned.

7 Trim the batik to size. Press, pin and zigzag stitch a double 1cm/½in turn-over down each long side and 2cm/¾in at the top and bottom. Nail the seat to the deckchair frame using upholstery pins. Start in the centre, then space the rest 2.5cm/1in apart.

Paint the background to this simple design using a homemade tool consisting of a cotton ball clipped into a clothes peg (pin). Scrunching the batik wax creates the distinctive vein-like batik lines.

Crackled Scarf

you will need

tracing paper and pencil

paper

silk pins (push pins)

lightweight silk, pre-washed

silk-painting frame

cotton balls

clothes pegs (pins)

iron-fix (set) silk paints

small bowls

medium and large artist's paintbrushes

batik wax

double boiler or wax pot

brown craft or lining paper

absorbent cloth or paper

iron

white spirit (turpentine) (optional)

needle

matching sewing thread

sewing machine (optional)

1 Trace the template at the back of the book on to paper. Pin the silk to a silk-painting frame and place it upside down over the design. Using a soft pencil, trace the design on to the back of the silk. This will reverse the design; if you want it to be the original way round, transfer it first on to tracing paper.

2 Make a large painting tool for each colour by clipping a cotton ball into a clothes peg (pin). Paint the base colours, which should be the palest in the design, on to the silk, allowing each one to dry before applying the next colour.

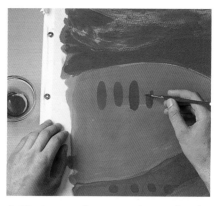

3 Using a medium artist's paintbrush, overpaint small areas of the pale base colours in a darker colour to start building up the design. Leave to dry.

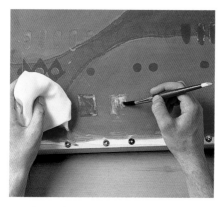

4 Heat the wax in a wax pot or a double boiler (see Techniques). Use a large artist's paintbrush to cover the central area of the silk with solid wax. Add details with the medium paintbrush. Leave to cool.

5 Remove the silk from the frame and scrunch the central waxed area to crack the surface. Replace the silk on the frame.

6 Using the large paintbrush, paint over the entire piece with the darkest colour, ensuring that it sinks into the cracks. Leave to dry.

7 Remove the fabric from the frame, place it between sheets of brown craft or lining paper, on top of an absorbent cloth or paper, and iron out the wax. Fix (set) the silk paints, following the manufacturer's instructions. Remove any remaining grease marks by soaking the fabric in white spirit (turpentine), then hand wash it in soapy water to remove the smell. Stitch a hem along the scarf edges.

Leather may seem an unusual material for batik, but you can crumple it in the same way as fabric to create the distinctive "cracked" effect. Use gum instead of wax, and special leather dyes.

Leather Book Cover

you will need

tracing paper, pencil and ballpoint pen

leather

cotton wool (cotton balls)

craft knife and cutting mat

brush

gum

rubber gloves

wool dauber (optional)

leather dyes, in yellow, red, green and black

soft cloth

board

spray adhesive (stencil mount)

mount board

leather lacquer spray

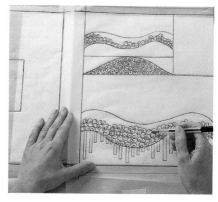

1 Trace the template at the back of the book. Dampen the leather with cotton wool (cotton balls), then transfer the design from the paper on to the leather. Cut out the leather for the book cover, using a craft knife and cutting mat. Leave the leather to dry. Brush the gum over the leather on the areas that will remain neutral.

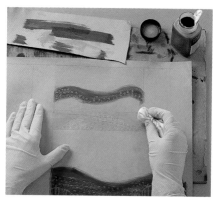

2 Wearing rubber gloves, dip a cotton wool pad or a wool dauber into the green dye. Press the pad on to a scrap of leather to remove any excess dye. Beginning in one corner, gently move the pad over the leather surface. Leave to dry naturally. Apply gum to those areas that will remain green. Repeat with the yellow dye.

3 Leave the green dye to dry naturally, and coat with gum in the same way. In turn, apply red dye to the leather with a cotton wool pad. When completely dry, block out with gum those areas that are to remain red or green.

4 Add the black in the same way. Crumple the leather to achieve a good "cracked" effect on the surface. Place the leather on a board and remove the gum with a large piece of damp cotton wool. Wash thoroughly with plenty of cold water.

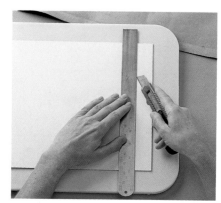

5 Bend and fold the leather into the desired shape while it is still damp. Mitre the corners. Leave to dry. Spray adhesive (stencil mount) on to the reverse side. Place a piece of mount board over the top and press the pieces together. Spray with lacquer.

This colourful abstract on black cotton was inspired by the artworks of Joan Miró. Test the cotton first to check that it is bleachable. Some wax remains in the fabric to keep it slightly stiff.

Modern Painting

you will need

tracing paper and pencil

thin paper

black pen

silk pins (push pins)

65 x 45cm/26 x 18in piece black cotton (bleachable), pre-washed

65 x 45cm/26 x 18in painting frame

masking tape

chalk

general-purpose wax

wax pot or double boiler

medium decorator's paintbrush

rubber gloves

bowls

bleach

vinegar

dye brush

dyes in red, yellow, orange, blue and green

iron

newspaper, brown or lining paper

sewing machine

black sewing thread

2 pieces of 1cm/⅜in dowelling, 50cm/20in long

fishing wire or string

1 Trace the template to the required size on to thin paper using a black pen. Pin the fabric to the frame, then tape the design on the back of the fabric. Hold the frame up to a light source and lightly trace the design on the front of the fabric, using chalk.

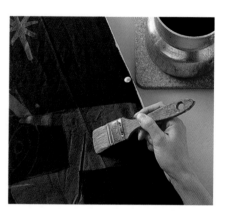

2 Heat the wax in a wax pot or double boiler (see Techniques). Apply it with a medium decorator's paintbrush to the areas that will remain black. Check that the wax has penetrated to the back of the fabric. If necessary, wax the same area from the back.

3 Remove the fabric from the frame. Wearing rubber gloves and working in a ventilated area, place the fabric in a bowl of thin bleach. Leave the fabric until it has turned cream, agitating it to allow even bleaching. Rinse in water, then rinse in water with a splash of vinegar to neutralize the bleach. Rinse in water again.

4 Pin the fabric back on the frame and leave it to dry. Check that the waxed lines are solid and re-wax any lines that are cracked. Using a dye brush, paint the dyes in the non-waxed areas, following the manufacturer's instructions. Leave to dry.

7 Hem both sides of the picture. Stitch a 2cm/¾in hem at the top and bottom. Insert a piece of dowelling at both ends. Attach a piece of fishing wire or string to both ends of the top piece of dowelling for hanging.

5 Apply wax to the coloured areas so that all the fabric is covered in wax. This is to avoid a wax shadow on the final picture. Remove the fabric from the frame.

6 Iron the fabric between sheets of newspaper, brown or lining paper. Continue ironing, replacing the paper until no more wax appears through. The cloth will remain slightly stiff.

This intricate batik design uses four different dye baths to build up the layers of colour. Chrome yellow, turquoise, peacock blue and navy make a stunning combination.

Abstract Cushion Cover

1 Cut one 47cm/18½in square and two 47 x 30cm/18½ x 12in rectangles of fabric. Enlarge the template from the back of the book on to a 41cm/16in square of paper and go over the lines with a felt-tipped pen. Trace the design on to the centre of the square.

3 For larger areas of the design, carefully outline them with the tjanting first, then fill them in using an old artist's paintbrush. Once all the white areas have been waxed, turn the frame over and, if necessary, re-wax any areas the wax has not penetrated completely. Leave to dry thoroughly.

2 Heat the wax in a wax pot or double boiler. Stretch the fabric square on to the tapestry frame and secure with drawing (push) pins. Use a tjanting to wax the areas you want to remain white. Use a pad of paper towels to prevent drips.

4 Prepare a yellow dye bath. Half fill a bucket with cold water, dissolve 30ml/2 tbsp of urea in 600ml/1 pint of lukewarm water. In a separate container mix 5ml/1 tsp of chrome yellow dye to a paste. Stir the urea solution into the dye paste and pour into the bucket. Dissolve 60ml/4 tbsp salt in 600ml/1 pint of lukewarm water and add to the bucket. Add the batik square and the rectangles, and stir for 6 minutes. Dissolve 15ml/1 tbsp of soda/sodium carbonate in a little warm water and add to the bucket. Leave the fabric to soak for 45 minutes, stirring occasionally. Remove and rinse in cold water until the water runs clear. Hang the fabric out to dry.

5 Apply wax to the areas that are to stay yellow.

6 Prepare a turquoise dye bath in the same way and immerse the fabric for 45 minutes. Rinse and dry it, then apply wax to the areas that are to remain green.

7 Prepare a blue dye bath with 10ml/ 2 tsp of dye, and leave the fabric in it for 1 hour. Rinse and dry the fabric, then wax the areas that are to remain blue. Plunge the fabric into cold water to crack the large areas of wax. Prepare another dye bath using 15ml/1 tbsp of navy dye. Leave the fabric to soak for several hours, then rinse and leave to dry.

8 Protect your ironing board with an old sheet. Place the batik between several layers of paper and iron over it to melt the wax. Keep replacing the newspaper until most of the wax has been removed. The last traces of wax can be removed by dry-cleaning or by immersing the fabric in boiling water. Press all the pieces while they are still damp.

9 Stitch a small hem along the long edge of each rectangle of fabric. Overlap the hems to make a 47cm/ 18½in square, right sides facing up, then pin and tack (baste) together.

10 With right sides together, pin the front and back of the cover together. Stitch around the outside edge of the batik. Trim the seams, clip the corners and turn right side out.

11 Remove the tacking threads. Ease out the corners and press the seams. Pin and stitch close to the inside edge of the border, and trim the threads. Sew a small piece of Velcro to the inside of the opening edges of the cover. Insert the cushion pad and close the Velcro.

Templates

Enlarge the templates on a photocopier. Alternatively, trace the design and draw a grid of evenly spaced squares over your tracing. Draw a larger grid on to another piece of paper and copy the outline square by square. Finally, draw over the lines to make sure they are continuous.

Silk Clock Face, p30–31

Indian Motif Shawl,
p36–37

Stained Glass Panel, p40–41

Summer Parasol, p28

Poppy Painting, p44–45

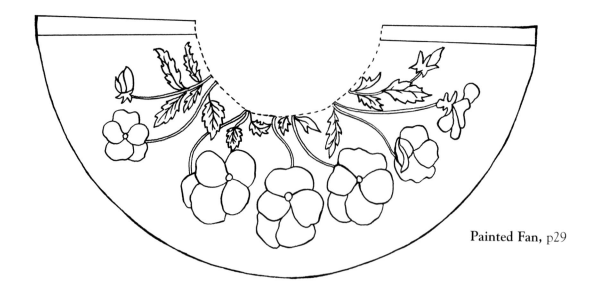

Painted Fan, p29

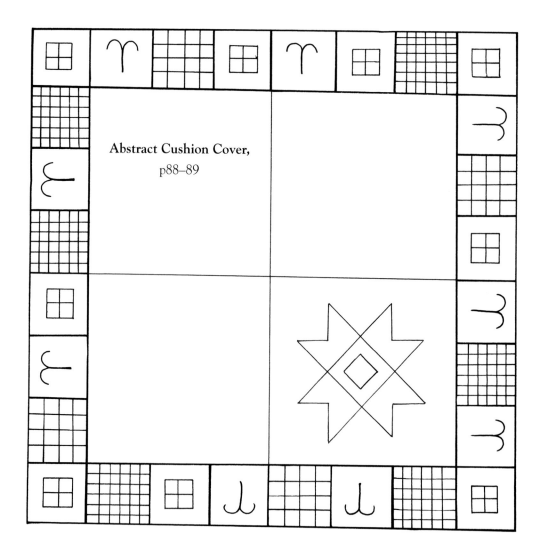

Abstract Cushion Cover,
p88–89

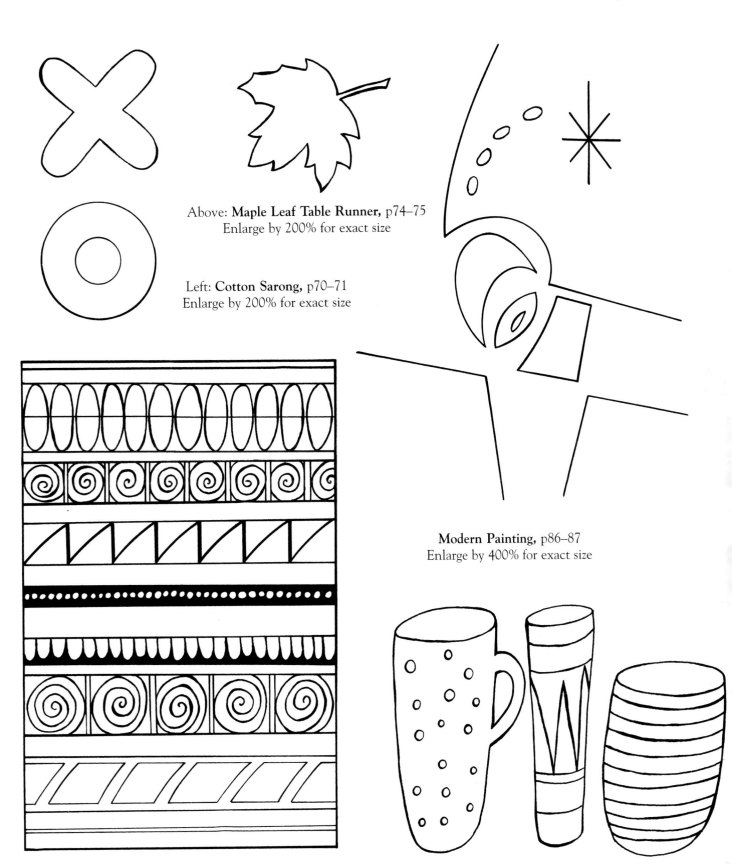

Above: **Maple Leaf Table Runner,** p74–75
Enlarge by 200% for exact size

Left: **Cotton Sarong,** p70–71
Enlarge by 200% for exact size

Modern Painting, p86–87
Enlarge by 400% for exact size

Bordered Scarf, p72–73
Enlarge by 200% for exact size

Quilted Table Mat, p66–7
Enlarge by 250% for exact size

Tiger Deckchair, p80–81
Enlarge by 500% for exact size

Square Silk Scarf, p68–69
Enlarge to 37.5cm/15in square for exact size

Silk Velvet Scarf,
p76–77
Enlarge by 200%
for exact size

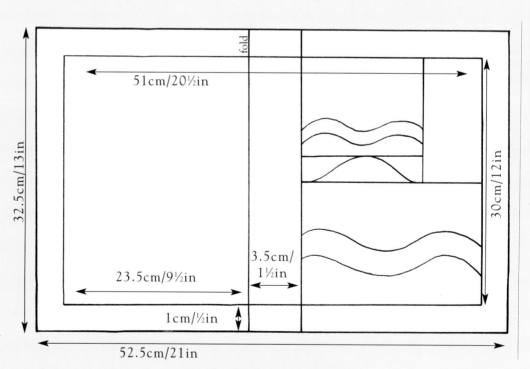

Leather Book Cover, p84–85

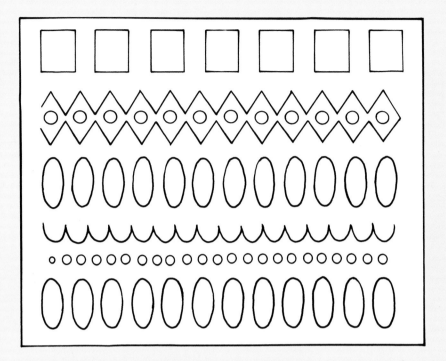

Crackled Scarf, p82–83

Stencilled Lily Scarf, p46

Flowery Camisole, p18–19

Patterned Seat Cover, p22–23

Acknowledgements

The publisher would like to thank the following people for designing projects in this book: **Ofer Acoo** for the Sunflower Cushion Cover p47. **Lucinda Ganderton** for the Abstract Picture Frame p24–25. **Helen Heery** for the Striped Silk Tie p64–65, Square Silk Scarf p68–69, Cotton Sarong p70–71 and Silk Velvet Scarf p76–77. **Sipra Majumder** for the Leather Book Cover p84–85.

Sarbjitt Natt for the Silk Clock Face p30–31 and Zodiac Scarf p43. **Sandra Partington** for the Stained Glass Panel p40–41 and Stencilled Lily Scarf p46. **Isabel Stanley** for the Flowery Camisole p18–19, Patterned Seat Cover p22–23, Summer Parasol p28, Polka Dot Kite p32, Indian Motif Shawl p36–37 and Resist-spotted Sarong p42. **Susie Stokoe** for the Salt-painted Tie p20–21, Salt-patterned Greetings Card p26–27, Painted Fan p29, Abstract Scarf p34–35, Poppy

Painting p44–45, Lightweight Folding Screen p58–59, Vibrant Silk Cushion Cover p60–61, Geometric Napkin p62–63, Quilted Table Mat p66–67, Bordered Scarf p72–73, Maple Leaf Table Runner p74–75 Crackle-finish Cosmetic Bag p78–79, Tiger Deckchair p80–81, Crackled Scarf p82–83 and Modern Painting p86–87. **Dorothy Wood** for the Abstract Cushion Cover p88–89.

Index